The No-State Solution

דאָרטן, וואָ מיר לעבען,
דאָרט איז אונזער לאַנד!

Wherever we live   that's our homeland

THE NO-STATE SOLUTION

A JEWISH MANIFESTO

DANIEL BOYARIN

Yale

UNIVERSITY PRESS

New Haven and London

Yale University Press books may be purchased in quantity for educational,
business, or promotional use. For information, please email sales.press@
yale.edu (U.S. office) or sales@yaleup.co.uk (U.K. office).

Set in Gotham and Adobe Garamond type by IDS Infotech, Ltd.
Printed in the United States of America.

Library of Congress Control Number: 2022938384
ISBN 978-0-300-25128-9 (hardcover : alk. paper)

A catalogue record for this book is available from the British Library.

This paper meets the requirements of ANSI/NISO Z39.48–1992
(Permanence of Paper).

10 9 8 7 6 5 4 3 2 1

Frontispiece art by Aharon Nisn Varady, adapted from a General Jewish
Labour Bund poster (Kiev, Ukraine, 1918), with an English translation of
the original Yiddish heading. For the poster, see wikimedia.org/wiki
/File:Bundposter1918.jpg.

Contents

Preface

After literally decades of obsessive thought about "the Jewish Question," I seem to have gotten myself into an aporia, a dead end of thinking with no way out. One way of describing this impasse would be that two of my most ardent political commitments—to full justice for Palestinians and to a vibrant, creative Jewish national culture— seem directly to contradict each other. It would seem as if the only way to fulfill the latter dream is to support the existence of the State of Israel, but clearly, the existence of the State of Israel makes the first dream impossible to fulfill. The forms, moreover, that this Jewish *national culture* takes in the Jewish state have always been problematical— inevitably so, I would argue, given the premises of such a state, even when pursued with the best will. This best will, furthermore, turns more and more sour almost by the day; it seems almost inevitably so. The nation-state is well on the way to being a racist, fascist state. Given the choice between justice and "my culture," "my nation," I have no choice but to choose justice, but the loss would be unsupportable. There is too much that I love, value, treasure, and enjoy deeply to become indifferent to the fate of the Jewish People and its works and days, and I have devoted *too much* of my life's work (not my career, but my life's work) to *Yiddishkayt* (Jewishness) to lose that struggle now. This loss would be for me not only unsupportable but virtually unthinkable. I am a Jew devoted to that predication and what it entails.

To frame this manifesto, I will begin with one of my first experiences of the dilemma. As a young teenager, I became deeply engaged with a Zionist socialist youth movement. What engaged me most (aside from the sheer excitement of militant involvement with comrades) were two aspects of the experience of the world it provided: a deep and thrilling absorption in Jewish history and culture, together with passionate desire that they continue, and an equal enthrallment with the idea of social justice for everyone: economic justice, cultural freedom, and equality for all the people and peoples of the world. The question of their relation was posed for me when the counselors informed us that the problem had been that too many Jews had been dedicated to universal social justice and not to the future of the Jews.

I bridled—to say the least. For me, a Jewish connection to progressive causes was a precious legacy of the Jewish folk itself. The implicit and explicit message of these Zionists was that the only way possible to advance these two ideals together, a rich and vibrant continuation of Jewish culture, and a universalist commitment to all the peoples of the world—except, it seems, to the Palestinians—was the State of Israel, where the Jews would control their own fate. So we were taught. I remained unconvinced. Nevertheless, they did convince me of the need for an equal and socially just world, and they instilled in me a passion for continued Jewish existence and, even more, for continued Jewish vitality in all spheres of creative life.

But during the two decades during which I dwelled, studied, taught, served in the Army Reserves, and with my wife raised a family in Israel, I gradually came to the realization that these two ideals were actually in deep tension with each other, even incompatible in the conditions of a Wilsonian single-culture-dominated state with citizens of other culture groups defined as resident aliens (at best) and systematically, if not generally violently—then—treated as second-class citizens, or worse. The occupation of the West Bank, Gaza, the

Golan, and Sinai only pointed up this impossible tension and contradiction even more. When I heard Yitzhaq Rabin say that the breaking of the arms and legs of children throwing stones was necessary to preserve the state, I repented of my erstwhile Zionism completely. Having evolved, then, during my years as an active citizen of the State of Israel into an active anti-Zionist, with, however, my commitment to Jewish identity and identification, Torah study, scholarship, practice, literature and liturgy, and modes of speech and thinking undiminished, even growing stronger and stronger, I have lived now for more than thirty years in the United States, experiencing the predicament ever more sharply: how can we remain a nation—for that is what I believe we are and should continue to be—and retain at the same time our absolute dedication to social justice for all?

As I will explore at some length in the manifesto that follows, at issue here is nothing less than what it means to be a Jew, and for some time now, that question has been answered in two ways: to be a Jew is to be either a member of a religion or of a nationality grounded in the existence of a nation-state. I reject both these answers.

What do the terms "religion" and "nation" mean? As I will be at some pains to demonstrate below, "religion" is notoriously difficult to define, but in its modern usage it almost always devolves to the essentially Protestant—even essentially Lutheran—notion of a belief system, disembedded from other forms of belonging, identity, and practice within a given nation. Such a view is embodied in English usage when we refer to "the Jewish faith," as if belief in certain propositions were what made one a Jew. One consequence of this distinction is that one may be removed from a religion by the powers that be for believing badly or not at all, or for heretical practices, while one belongs to a nation whatever one's beliefs. As such, if the Jews are a "religion," we can have Jews who belong to many nations. Nations have members; states have citizens. On that view, which I don't share, of course, one could be a Jew and also a member of some other nation: be a Jew at home and an Englishman abroad.

For some time, I have tried to show how the term "religion," implying a "faith" and a sphere of life separated from kinship, politics, and economics, is inappropriate historically, particularly for the Jews, as well as for most folks in the world. "Judaism" as the name of a "faith" or "religion" is a new invention, a new usage, especially among Jews ourselves. "The Jews," then, is not the name of a religion, and the Jews, historically, at any rate, are not a religion.[1]

The alternative, "nation," is somewhat less problematic from a historical point of view, for while there is no native Jewish term for "religion"—*dat*, the current term translating "religion," being a very recent development in that sense—the term *'am* goes back to the Bible, and while perhaps not perfectly translated as "nation," comes pretty close, and so I will try to show below that the Jews manifest many of the characteristics usually assigned to nations, such as shared narratives of origins and trials and tribulations, shared practices (including, but not limited to, "cultic" practices), shared languages, and other cultural forms. One further consequence of the nation, as currently imagined, is that it is taken to imply, in addition to the factors just mentioned, shared territory and power over that territory, a territory just for "us," whoever "us" are: here, we speak of Jews.

Consequently, my insistence on the Jews as nation has elicited, quite understandably, the question, sometimes hostile, less often friendly—"So you've become a Zionist?" It seems at first glance—again—that the only answer to the question of "If not a religion, then what"? is "A nation." Since, moreover, "we [allegedly] all know that a nation means a state," our commitment to continued Jewish cultural vitality seems to lead right back to Ben Gurion National Airport, aghast at what we see. I have *not*, needless (or needful) to say, become a Zionist. Right now, in the here and now, for reasons to be explored in some detail below, it is a very bad idea for Jews to claim the status of "religion." I have decided I can no longer live with this dead end, but I must avoid the paved roads that both lead to perdition and find another way forward, however rocky the road ahead. What is to be done?

I have been living with this dilemma, striving to be a "good Jew" in the ethical sense of passion for the well-being of others who are not Jews— especially those wronged by the Jews themselves, the Palestinians— while at the same time loving and caring for my people and their "doings," studying Talmud, keeping the Sabbath, speaking Yiddish, dancing with Kurdish or Yemenite Jews, and studying their Torah together with that of Ashkenazic (northern European) Jews. I have been thinking rather obsessively about these questions for decades now, resigned to just living in a dead end; now I'm searching for a way through. The impetus for my renewed energy comes from a challenge that recently came my way in very sharp tones indeed: "What do you mean when you say 'Jews'? You deny the existence of 'Judaism,' so what is the meaning of 'Jews'?" I cannot escape; I cannot desist. As the Talmud itself says: "It is not your obligation to finish the task, but neither are you free to desist from engaging in it" (Pirke Avot 2). I know that my answers have holes in them, deep flaws, but I hope, nonetheless, that we have here a beginning, the start of a way to find a Northwest Passage through the pack ice, perhaps a "lead," a crack in the ice that conducts to a way out.[2]

We can't go on, but we must go on.

Let me now introduce the major points of the "no-state solution" that I will be expounding in the coming chapters of this manifesto. The source of the dilemma is what I take to be a gross and fateful error that is itself compounded of two errors. The first of these errors, as I've said, is the assumption that there are only two alternatives for

Jewish self-definition (self-fashioning): either we imagine ourselves and conduct ourselves as a "religion," eschewing all the forms of national existence, or we define ourselves as a "nation," with a national religion and multiple other forms of cultural practice that may only, or certainly best, be fulfilled in the context of a sovereign Jewish nation-state. Supposedly, it's one or the other: religion (no state) or nation (necessarily implicating a state; that is, Zionism). I'm going to be offering, explaining, and defending a newish proposition, a third position: that the Jews are a diaspora nation. I hope to show, or at least make plausible, the idea that it is a serious error to argue that the Jews are just a religion in order to avoid affirming the Jewish nation-state and that it is possible to imagine nations without states, not as an anomaly or deficiency, but as a significantly better way to organize human/Jewish cultural vitality without sacrificing the claims for universal justice.

I categorically reject the nation-state solution to the continuity of Jewish existence and culture in favor of a diasporic nationalism that offers not the promise of security, but rather the highly contingent possibility of an ethical collective existence. Indeed, I oppose the mononational state itself—for all—as a proven dangerous and destructive mode of collective life. While the argument here is primarily focused on the Jews, I invite all others into the conversation; perhaps there is something here to be fought for or against by everyone. I do not expect the argument to be welcomed eagerly by all. So be it: the no-state solution, the Diaspora Nation.

My text is written in a style that is—I am learning—not only strange but somewhat off-putting, or at any rate difficult for many readers. It is not intended to be difficult, but it is intended to be what it is, so perhaps a few words of explanation will ease the way. My "ideas," such as they are, are a product of constant reading, dialoguing (in my head), getting excited by and learning from or being appalled by and learning from the writings of others. The ideas don't float in a universe of their own; each one is rooted, still, in a conversation. I reproduce some of the conversations here; without them, there is no structure, no depth to the ideas. These conversations locate the ideas as "authentic" in the sense that they have been articulated by folks, mostly Jews, before. They form threads in a woven text/ile or, in another metaphor, small pieces of glass in a mosaic, retaining their own integrity and also contributing to the whole picture. There would be no color or texture to the manifesto if its origin in a web of previous expressions and encounters or its place in a new mosaic of my making were obscured.

The style of reading indicated by such a style of writing might be termed talmudic, and, given my formation, not surprisingly so. Thought here is developed out of commentary on texts and on disputation with them and among them. This mode of thinking and writing of producing and communicating new/old thoughts has been termed "textual reasoning."[3] The thoughts and ideas bruited here are products not of my head but of my deep and ongoing conversations with interlocutors living and dead. They are, moreover, deeply rooted in traditional Jewish ways of thinking, from the Talmud to the Yiddish Socialist Bund and beyond. I welcome you, the reader, to my textual reasoning. It may make your reading more difficult, surely less smooth and sure, and even slow you down, but I hope the work will be worth it. I endeavor to the best of my ability to avoid putting obstacles in your path, because I desire, fervently, that you understand what I am saying here, even if and when you continue to disagree.

Readers may garner from this more of an idea of why I write the way I do: citing, disagreeing, agreeing "but," adding and subtracting to citations of those whose words I respect, and out of that process developing what may be called "my" ideas.

INTRODUCTION
The New Jewish Question

The people called "the Jews" seems to find itself in an intractable conflict over self-identification at this point in its historical existence, a cloud of unknowing just what "the Jews" means and what it is. The way that this discord is usually phrased goes something like: Are "the Jews" (aka Jewry) a "religion" or a "nation"?[1]

SPEAKER J: The Jews are a religion; they are not a nation and don't need a state.

SPEAKER Z: No, the Jews are not a religion; the Jews are a nation, and a nation must have a state.

These are the terms of a scorching—very angry—debate going on among Jews and about Jews for much of the twentieth century and even now. Note how the crucial issue of Zionism comes up on both sides of this argument. Both Zionists and anti-Zionists seem to agree that it is only by defining the Jews as a "religion," and not a "nation," that the inexorability of a "Jewish state"—with all that implies for all of the inhabitants of Palestine—can be avoided. Both of these choices, however, seem both inapt and inept, at least for achieving the goals of my interrogation.

The name "religion" seems not to entail any particular historical, linguistic, or cultural indices or identifications, but rather a set of beliefs and practices conditioned by those beliefs, just as "religion" functions in a world of particularly Protestant Christianity.[2] The name "nation," on the other hand, seems to imply a shared history, material culture, language and literature, and, above all else, sovereignty, a land to call one's own, whether existing now or merely aspired to and longed for.[3] In the case of the Jews, then, naming us a religion seems at first glance to allow uniquely for a non-Zionist Jewish imagination of ourselves, our collective identity—we are all the people in the world who believe that there is an Oral Torah given at Sinai that we are bound to obey, or something similar—there's nothing to say about a collective politics at all. Naming us a nation, by contrast, implies a collective politics without necessitating any particular set of beliefs about G-d or anything else of a supernatural cast. Since the nation, it is claimed, must be sovereign in order to be a nation, if the Jews are a nation, then, according to the regnant view, nothing but a nation-state, the State of Israel, could fulfill their/our historical destiny. This is the situation we find on all sides, among both supporters and detractors of the Jewish state. From this follows the insistence on Jewish nationhood on the part of Zionists and the utter resistance to this status by anti-Zionists.

What Does "What Is?" Mean?

My original title proposed for this book was *What Is the Jews?* Alas, the grammar constabulary wouldn't let me do that. I cite it here because it is an important element in my construction herein. Before I get any further into attempting to answer the question posed by that lost title, I would do well to explain it or at least to unpack it. The two pieces of the question about the question both hang on the words "What is?" and the answers to them come together. First of all, then, why do I write (perversely, some would say), "What is the Jews?" and not "What are the Jews?" The answer is that I am writing not of a collection of individuals who either call themselves or are called by others, or both, "Jews," but am asking about a collective identity. I could ask, "What is the Jewish nation?" and no one would blink a grammatical eyelash, but since "nation" is one of the possible answers to my question, I can't do that. Another possibility would be "What is Jewry?", which in many ways might seem the most satisfactory, but could feel quite archaic and stilted to some. The point is that I am asking about a social entity and inquiring how that entity is best described. That entity is named "the Jews," so instead of saying, "How is the entity called 'the Jews' best described?", I've abridged it to "What is the Jews?" As a recent account of the philosophy of social groups asks: "Is a social group distinct from the collection of people who are its members, and if so, how is it different?"[4] I am assuming that the social group—at any rate, the one called the Jews—is different from the collection of people, Jews, who are its members, and therefore I ask: What is this social group? There are, after all, many types of social groups, ones characterized by aspects of appearance (race), place of dwelling (states), doings and sayings (religions), biological differences (sexes, or do I mean genders?), practices (queer). What is the Jews— a race, a nation, a religion, a gender, a sexuality?

It seems that the first three of that list have been and remain strong contenders but, perhaps surprisingly, even the last two have appeared in definitions of Jewry from outside, especially the male Jew as a woman or the "Jew" as queer.[5] But we can still query: What are we asking when we ask if Jewry, for instance, is a "nation" or a "religion"? As we've already seen above, the stakes can be high, especially the political stakes; much rides on this question, having crucial repercussions in the lives of several million people, and not only Jews. In the quite recent past, and in many quarters even now, many of the types of social groupings I have just named are understood (either explicitly or, perhaps more often, tacitly) as real things in the world, real categories of the likes of "dogs," "trees," or even "tables." So the "races" of so-called man have been taken as really existing and definite divisions.[6] "Religion" and "religions" were held to have existed always and everywhere wherever there are humans. Once, not too long ago, even "nations" were so understood as well. We could call these categories, as they were understood, "natural" categories: "religions" and "nations" like "trees" or "birds."

Over the last century or so, these assumptions have come under question. First of all, "nation" has been exposed as a modern construct, and many of the seemingly most solid of national foundations have been shown to be products of early modernity. France, Italy, and even that most assertive of national groups, Germany, have all been produced as entities (not only political entities) within the last three hundred years or so.[7] Over the decades, most of those other social categories have fallen like trees as well. Anthropological research, for one thing, has shown how culturally specific they are: most of the cultures of the world, both in the past and in the present, have no category of "religion" as a separate entity, a separate sphere within social or cultural life.[8] This is not to claim that many have no gods or rituals or myths, but only that these practices or doings don't form a separate, distinct category in their worldview or their lives, as they do in Euro-America, and there, again, only since early modernity. These categories are social constructs, as we tend to say now; that is, they exist only because a given group of humans name the category and name themselves among its members, so "religion" exists only where folks talk about it or something very much like it as a category; the category of nations exists only within linguistic/cultural/conceptual systems that recognize it, and so on. "Judaism" did not exist for Jews until Jews started using the term or its cognates and equivalents in languages other than English; the Jews did not exist as a "nation" until the category of nations had been produced.[9]

One response to the idea of social groupings as constructs is simply to deny their existence and significance entirely, so when I claim that both religions and nations are fairly modern conceptual coinages, then the question, those responders might argue, of whether the Jews is a nation or a religion is meaningless, since neither of those categories exist in reality. As philosopher Katherine Ritchie has written, "The scoffing social constructionist claims that like goblins, mermaids, and dragons, racial identities, nations, and money are fictional," with the consequence that "if social construction means unreal or nonexistent, there are no identity groups to band around in social justice or national projects." However, another view of "social construction," also formulated by Ritchie, claims that "if social groups figure in true explanations, they exist and are important in understanding our world and working to make it a more just place."[10]

I favor the latter—nonscoffing—interpretation, because it allows for concerted activity to reduce or enhance the currency and power of a particular construction. Not all forms of social grouping are salutary. "Race" may have functioned until now—usually adversely—but demonstrations that there are no biological "races" may increasingly disable those adverse effects in the future. The same is true of "nations." Likewise for "religions." The question is what is gained and, just as significantly, what is lost, if we destroy one or another of these two categories.

I begin with what I take to be a real object, a human group, a collective that does things and to which things are done and I ask what is the best way to describe it, both historically (that is, in the past) and normatively (that is, in the future). This is a delicate balance to maintain. On the one hand, the normative implies a desired change from something in the present to something else. The present, moreover, has no more (or less) normative claim than any previous state of affairs. The contention is rather that insofar as there are elements of the present that seem to me to be wrong, bad for the Jews (and for everyone else), morally and ethically compromising (or worse), they are at least partly based on misinterpretations of the past and its norms. There are, furthermore, possibilities that have been hidden or forgotten in the past that are attractive and can be revitalized in the establishment of new norms.

Caveat Emptor: No Utopia Here

To live outside the law, however, you must be honest.[11] As English literary critic Stefan Collini recently argued in the *Times Literary Supplement*: "Using some selected elements from the past to support a case in the present is an entirely legitimate enterprise, but a tricky one: if the historical foundations are shaky, the polemical superstructure starts to look wobbly, too."[12] I am proposing here an old-new mode of existence for the Jews going forward, founded—I aspire—in good scholarship on the past, acknowledging to the best of my ability where the elements I have selected need at least some shoring up in the recognition of some cracks in the foundation. In other words, I hope not to hide or ignore elements of the past that do not fit with my manifesto for the future. In harmony with my own normative enterprise (or polemic) here and its relation to history, Amnon Raz-Krakotzkin writes: "I argue that concealed within the very concept of exile resides the potential for a comprehensive viewpoint that allows for a different relation with the various forms of Jewish-Israeli collectivity. It is possible to dredge up 'exile' from past interpretations through to its current development and develop its idea as a general ethical-cultural position that enables a Jewish self-definition turning toward those same denied foundations of the present, and which enables their open existence and recognizes their point of view."[13] What would render the enterprise both rhetorically wobbly and intellectually/ethically questionable would be simply to ignore history that goes against one's ideological perspective.

This book is not intended as an apologetic. I am sharply critical of certain aspects of Jewish cultural history and traditional ideology, including of course those tendencies that contribute to Zionism. While seeking, as I've just said, strenuously not to be apologetic—or, still less, chauvinist—myself, I cannot get away without mentioning prominently right here in the introduction chauvinist representations that have been very conspicuous in various kinds of historical Jewish discourse, notably, the binary division of humanity into Jews and "goyim." I will try not to attempt to explain these away. I trust, however, that they may be detoxified somewhat by contextualization and transmutation and thus rendered less poisonous in the present.

These unfortunate faces of *Judaïté* have been most recently exposed in the work of Adi Ophir and Ishay Rosen-Zvi in a monograph very straightforwardly entitled *Goy*.[14] In this genealogy, the authors demonstrate how a relatively uncharged word in biblical Hebrew, simply meaning something like "nation," in which Israel can be comprehended as a "goy," becomes transformed historically to mean all who are *not* Israel. In the meantime, the word, which had been collective, becomes singular, so that an individual non-Jew becomes a "goy" themselves, giving finally the modern and frequently contemptuous "goy" for an individual, and the plural, "goyim"—which had earlier meant "nations"—now as the plural of individual non-Jews. Israel, moreover, somehow had exited from the family of nations. I am not going to repeat here even in précis the brilliant, erudite, and compelling argument of Rosen-Zvi and Ophir or attempt a historical contextualization (inevitably apologetic) of those developments, but I do mark here what negative effects this has had on the vaunted (and also itself potentially chauvinistic) commitment of Jews to justice for all, especially when integrated with the doctrines of chosenness.

I agree with such writers as Ophir and Rosen-Zvi, as well as many others less articulate, perhaps, than they, that strong, dark currents of chauvinism have blown in the winds of the Jewish imagination for centuries. Those winds also are part of the inspiration for Zionism and for some, at least, of its worst practices. As I write (May 2021), this chauvinism is rearing its ugliest head. In Israel, kangaroo courts composed only of Jews—or virtually so—have decided that neighborhoods where Palestinians have lived for generations, many able to produce deeds to prove it, are *really* "Jewish lands." Their houses are being taken away by force in state-supported pogroms, while racist, fanatic settlers toss out the Palestinian inhabitants and their goods (except for what the settlers want to keep) and move their families in. I do not claim that Zionism devised such forces among Jews; they have been latent and sometimes manifest forever.

Back to the Future

To return to my main argument, putting it somewhat crassly, I am interested here in "real Jews," Jews who live and breathe, eat and make love and get pregnant (or don't), get sick and die and, on the way, behave in various ways: singing, dancing, writing books, reading books, speaking quaint languages, and arguing constantly. How shall we describe them, and what are the consequences of doing so? We can ask as a historical question whether the Jews constituted a "religion" or a "nation" or a "race" in the past; these are answerable. What the Jews was may be an empirical or partly empirical question. What the

Jews will be or ought to be is something else. Whether or not the categories of the Jews as a religion or as a nation came into being only in the last couple of centuries, not to mention "Jewish Peoplehood," which is a century old, the question is whether they are useful or harmful now and in the future, or whether should we strive to do away with them.[15] This is the new Jewish Question. Ritchie helpfully summarizes her analysis of identity groups, putting forth that "in seeking to understand identity, our options are not that identity groups are fictions or that they are biologically defined categories. Social identity groups exist. They are non-fictional entities rooted in complex networks of social relations. . . . Identity groups are socially constructed because their natures are social."[16] What kind of social identity do we *want* for the Jews? It's a question of values. Assuming that many of the readers of this manifesto share values with me, they may find my answer here helpful in realizing those values.

Identification of what the Jews were or what they were not has been advanced as a knockdown argument for what they should be. On the one hand, if one could demonstrate the modernity of a concept such as the Jews constituting a nation, it has seemed possible to discredit Jewish nationalism, along with its alleged inevitable coconspirator Zionism. A good example of this contention can be found in the highly popular writing of an Israeli historian, Shlomo Sand, in *The Invention of the Jewish People*, a book that has been read by hundreds of thousands of people in several countries and languages by now.[17] Reading him carefully and critically will help to articulate the problems of ideas such as his, which are quite widely held and thus important to deal with.

Sand writes with a fair measure of cocksureness that "Judaism was simply an appealing religion that spread widely until the triumphant rise of its rivals, Christianity and Islam, and then, despite humiliation and persecution, succeeded in surviving into the modern age."[18]

However, his formulation completely ignores the last century of scholarship exposing problems with the concept of religion and its own historical construction as a category.[19] He does not attempt to articulate what a "religion" is, where one comes from, who spreads or promulgates one, or why Christianity and Islam are rivals, and not perhaps forms of that same "appealing religion." In short, while being hypercritical of the notion of a people or nation, Sand simply accepts the most run-of-the-mill, unexamined versions of the notion of a religion and assumes they have always and everywhere just been there. If it were only Sand, it would not justify me asking you to spend time reflecting on this kind of thought and the problems it raises, but his views are typical, even though his version of them is particularly extreme.

Sand uses their formulation to take a relatively liberal position. He wishes to counter the idea that Jews are connected and separated by ties of "blood," which is to say that the Jews are a "nation-race." He desires to defeat this doctrine that, according to him, asserts the existence of particular Jewish blood or, more recently, Jewish genes and the "racial homogeneity" of all Jews. Moreover, according to him, that racist doctrine generates the inability of Israel to be a state "that accepts its diversity while serving its inhabitants."[20] In other words, for Sand, the very idea that the Jews form a "nation" or even a "people," as opposed to a church, inevitably implies the crudest forms of racism, with its fascist state forms. Furthermore, Sand seems to accept, as nearly everyone does, the conviction that nation is identical to nation-state. It is the idea of Jews as a nation, even a race, that, according to Sand, makes it impossible for the Israeli state to be a democracy, a state for all of its citizens. Since the only alternative to the national idea, he thinks, lies once again in the by-him uninterrogated category of a "belief-culture," which he understands "religion" to be, then that is what the Jews must be in order not to be proponents of an ethnocratic, racist nation-state.

It is, perhaps, time for me to put some cards on the table. As should be clear, I disagree with Sand's book and with the ideology that he represents, namely, the idea that only by reducing *Yiddishkayt* to a "religion," a faith with no national character, is it possible to avoid the consequences of statism. I disagree with him in his contention that racist ideas and the idea that each ethnic group has the right to a state just for them are *necessary* consequences of nationalism, however frequently they may accompany the latter. Yet politically and ethically, I find myself on the same side of the table as Sand. I agree with him that racist notions of biological homogeneity among Jews and of the state as belonging to all Jews and only Jews are anathema; indeed, the idea of a Jewish state altogether appalls me. I am against the ideas set out by neo-Zionist ideological state apparatuses and non-state apparatuses of the national exclusivity of the state. I claim that such a doctrine is always pernicious, since in its liberal form, "others" are merely tolerated, while in its illiberal forms, they are not even that. I believe, with Sand, that those ideas, that ideology, almost necessarily leads to Israeli discourse rapidly growing more and more racist, along with the discourses of supporters of Israel around the world.

As I've said, one of the consequences of conflating nation with state is that myriad Zionists and anti-Zionists alike arrive at the logical inference: if not a religion, then a nation, and if a nation, then the State of Israel. That logic abounds in Zionist imaginations: operating with these dichotomies and confusing anti-Semitism with anti-Zionism, a sitting judge on the Pennsylvania Supreme Court recently delivered himself of the following opinion (or perhaps obiter dictum):

> The Hellenization phenomenon is embodied in the idea of "good Jews" and "bad Jews." The "good Jews" distance themselves from Zionism and Israel. They embrace the cause of any persecuted minority group other than the Jewish people.

They become ashamed of being Jewish and enlist themselves in every cause except that of Jews. The "bad Jews" insist on the value of Jewish heritage, on Zionism, on Ahavat Yisrael (love of one's fellow Jews), and on being proud to be Jewish and identifying as Jewish. I'm trying to give my own characterization of this dichotomy, which is imperfect, but I think very telling.[21]

The proudly self-named "bad Jew" Justice David Wecht, "bad" from the point of view of the "Hellenizing" liberals that he fantasizes, cannot comprehend the possibility that one might insist on the value of Jewish heritage, on Ahavat Yisrael, and on self-identifying as Jewish—and still reject "Zionism." For such as Wecht, that is the only possible referent and outcome of Jewish nationhood.

What, then, shall we call a collective that shares language forms, historical memories, ancient and modern literatures, practices of time and space, stories and customs? I believe that such a human grouping is best called a "nation," but only if we can redeem it from its nearly ubiquitous recent misuse. "Peoplehood," often offered as an alternative, reeks to me of neoliberalism, of highly problematic discourses of inclusion and exclusion (of "racial" minorities within Jewry, of dissident genders and sexualities, of nonbreeders in general), of an unhealthy focus on natality as virtually the only marker of the continuity of the Jewish People, as well as of virtually meaningless identification as a sign of success. I can think of nothing but "nation" (as it was used almost to the end of the nineteenth century and still at many sites as a name for a collective and not a sovereignty or territory). I hope that this book will help educate Judge Wecht, because I hope in this manifesto to demonstrate a very different—aspirationally nontoxic—way of thinking about nationalism, and Jewish nationalism in particular. First, however, I'd like to show why I reject a seemingly, at first glance, alternative view, one that dismisses separate cultural identities nearly entirely: cosmopolitanism.

Against Cosmopolitanism: A Density of Overlapping Allegiances

In the time this extended essay searching for a model for an ethical and vital continuation of the Jewish People was being prepared, I have been surprised—almost shocked—at a furious response to the project that has come from various quarters and in various forms, namely, vehement opposition to any meaningful continuation of Jewish collectivity at all. I had expected fury from the Right, but hardly from the Left, and have had to think hard where it comes from. There are, so it seems to me, two basic reasons why people "of goodwill" continue to think that the Jews should not persist as a collective, even if most of these people do not take the time to articulate to themselves that they do think that and even if they are unaware of these two reasons. One is the lingering and still very much potent doctrine of Christian supersessionism—the idea that with the new revelation, Jewish particular existence is now obsolete. This doctrine, as has been shown in various works of postcolonial criticism (for example, by Jonathan Boyarin, Aamir Mufti, Kathleen Biddick, and Kathleen Davis), deeply informs modern colonial ideologies of Eurocentric progressivism. The fact that it also informs the implicit attitudes of critical people of goodwill shows how effective it remains.

The second is the still-potent doctrine that the peoples and land of the world are best and "rightly" divided up into ethnic nation-states, and therefore the only way to oppose Zionism is to oppose the very idea of the Jews as a nation or even a people. Indeed, much of the animus against the persistence of the Jews as a collective (and endless amounts of confusion) centers on the effort of Jews and others to "solve the Jewish problem" by creating a Jewish nation-state—a solution that has been in many ways disastrous for Jewishness and for others. In the nineteenth and twentieth centuries, this has often led to the charge that Jews who continue to manifest their distinctive identity, even when they have the opportunity to shed it, are engaging in an unwarranted (and, some would suspect, characteristic) clannishness, whereas no one would suspect, for example, a teacher native to and resident in Montpellier or even a Francophone resident of, for instance, Martinique, of clannishness for focusing on and promoting the continuation of French literature. The effectiveness of these two factors (supersessionism and territorial nationalism) to inform prejudice against collective Jewish continuity is perhaps mitigated when Jews per se are obviously the objects of collective discrimination and correspondingly exacerbated when Jews as a collective appear to be "powerful" or secure.

To be sure, arguments against "identity politics" have been offered on other and more sympathetic grounds as well. Cultural historian Walter Benn Michaels has argued that inevitably, any ascription of group identity to genealogy is ipso facto racialized and even racist in essence.[22] Michaels argues that all conceptions of cultural ethnicity are dependent on prior and often unacknowledged notions of race. In a series of examples, Michaels contends that those who insist they are talking only about culture and not something that is biologically innate nevertheless assume that someone who does not "have" the culture of his or her "people" is in some sense lacking something and that the lack can be repaired. Michaels questions this assumption: if they do not already observe the practices of that culture, in what sense other than "racial" can it be said to be theirs?[23] His conclusion: "This is not to say, of course, that all accounts of cultural identity require a racial component; it is only to say that the accounts of cultural identity that do any cultural work require a racial component."[24] By this he means that one is already either doing "Navajo doings" or not. If one is doing them, then there is no cultural work to be done; they are one's culture already. If one is not already doing them, then it can make sense to call them one's culture only on the basis of an assumed or imputed biological identity as Navajo. He concludes that "the modern concept of culture is not, in other words, a critique of racism; it is a form of racism."[25]

Michaels's argument that any identification of culture with ethnicity is logically dependent on a genealogical connection for it to work seems at first glance correct, and it would seem to condemn any effort to promote consanguinity and "family" as a basis of an identity to the charge of racism. Yet by calling "racist" all claims for group identity based on genealogy, he inscribes a particular ideology of identity as natural and renders all others as somehow unnatural.

His is a radically individualist, voluntaristic, and attenuated notion of something that can only with difficulty be called "identity." The valorization of any kind of elective and affective connection between people over against the claims of physical kinship is deeply embedded in the Platonic value system that Europe has largely inherited from Paul. In opposition to a traditional Jewish culture which, in virtually all of its varieties, considered literal descent from Abraham and thus physical kinship as of supreme value in establishing identity, Paul preached kinship in the spirit as the mark of identity. In addition, where other Jewish groups insisted on the value of doing traditional Jewish things—the Law—as the practice of Jewish identity, Paul asserted the doing of new things, "better" things, baptism, for instance, as the marker of Christian identity. Both of these moves are founded on the hierarchical dualism of spirit and flesh, with anything having to do with flesh implicitly and explicitly devalued.[26]

Identity is not only reinvented, as Michaels would have it; it is at least partially given for different people in different ways and intensities. Bodies are marked as different and often as negatively different from the dominant cultural system, thus producing a dissonance or gap between one's practices and affects. Contact with other people who share the name of a given identity and seem to feel organically connected to a community can produce a sense of nostalgia, even in one who has never participated in the things that community does. Michaels obscures all of this by eliding racism—the idea of an innate capacity or tendency for certain practices—and generation, understood as a kinship with other people who happen to do certain things. Versions of this same argument can be constructed for all of Michaels's deconstructions of so-called culturalism.

I should probably clarify here in no uncertain terms: when I speak of "Jewish continuity," I am *not* speaking of ensuring that large numbers of babies be born who are the children of two at least nominally Jewish parents, as does so much of the neoliberal American Jewish establishment.[27] I mean something else entirely: the continued critical, creative development of Jewish cultural practices. Jewish identity is not the issue, nor, even less, Jewish pride. Jewish culture can confer shame, and identity without critical content can be itself shameful.

My struggle here and throughout my life is to find ways of thinking and acting, writing and speaking, that enable the quite wonderful, lively intimacy of diasporic Jewish life without activating or even managing to suppress the latent and too often manifest sense of superiority that may have been sustaining under conditions of repression, but that can only itself constitute such conditions on others now. Let me give one example. In the Diaspora, Jews developed a custom of spitting as they passed a church (if no one was looking), a response understandable perhaps when the Catholic Church was the major instigator of all manner of violence against Jews. This was a kind of Jewish guerilla movement. Such behavior, perhaps understandable then, is inexcusable with respect to mosques and indeed churches now wherever Jews are not persecuted and especially when they are in power.

Instead of Jewish pride—whatever that might mean, but I'm sure it's not good—I propose Jewish pleasure, Jewish joy.[28] The intimacies of shared history, languages, practices, songs, holy days, literature, political comradeship (Black Lives Matter), things we eat *and things we don't eat*, and even perhaps the joys of transgression, all the things that add up to my most outrageous coinage, *Jewissance*, I offer as a replacement for the contemptuous and negative tendencies of discourses of Jews as elect and dividing the world into Jews and goyim. I see no contradiction whatever between commitment to one's nation's past and traditions and welfare together with conationals and even caring a bit more for "one's own" and an equally passionate commitment to the well-being of the entire world, especially through local activism and solidarity.

Here I propose an argument for an *ethical* form of *vibrant* Jewish collective continuity.[29] It simply rejects the theology of supersessionism, arguing that there is no reason why Jews have more or less right to collective existence than any other what I call here *nation*—a complex term whose implications I will unpack throughout this book. It also strives toward as its sine qua non justice, inclusiveness, and human well-being for Jews and everyone, lately including octopuses, as well.

Cosmopolitanism, by contrast, offers itself as an alternative to the claim for an ethical political life with others. In cosmopolitanism, each individual belongs only to himself (I use the pronoun advisedly) and thus is, as the name translates, a citizen and member only of the world community of humans. I decline cosmopolitanism as the solution to the Jewish Question (and most others) for reasons that I will develop now at some length.

In order that I might not be misunderstood, let me emphasize here that I refer by this term to what philosopher Martha Nussbaum has called "the very old idea of the cosmopolitan," namely, sole "allegiance . . . to the worldwide community of human beings."[30] Analysis of the writing of one of the most prominent espousers of this idea of cosmopolitanism, not quite but almost "disembodied universalism," Professor Kwame Anthony Appiah, illustrates precisely the flaws of the cosmopolite solution to the evident horrors generated by nationalism understood as territorialism. Appiah lays out a philosophy of cosmopolitanism that essentially proposes a "universal morality," common to all peoples, or at any rate applicable to all peoples.[31] Although Appiah is much more sophisticated than English missionaries of the nineteenth century, one still suspects that his "objective moral 'truths' " will, *mirabile dictu*, conform to those of Oxbridge moral philosophers. And indeed, in his public practice as the "Ethicist" of the *New York Times*, it certainly would appear that he conceives of morality as universal. This cosmopolitanism ends up having the effect (perhaps unintended; let's give the benefit of the doubt) of wiping out any significance of cultural differences, substituting for them that universal standard. This cosmopolitanism amounts to—again, perhaps without intent—supersessionism writ very large indeed.

If I've understood Appiah, he argues that to hold a value is to desire that all will hold it, and therefore it follows that those who have more power have the right to call the tune (since he seems to agree that there is no way to judge values that is not tied to "who you are").[32] He explicitly says, "From the fact that beliefs are subjective in this way, therefore, it does not follow that they are subjective in the sense that you are *entitled* to make any judgements you like." Unfortunately, the upshot is that it is the British colonials who *are* entitled to make the judgments of what judgments are legitimate and what are not, and not the Indian natives. (Presumably it is a tenet of universal morality that some folks have the right to go to where other folks live and by exercise of firepower or economic power simply impose their values on those others as universals.) Anthropologists are *not* cosmopolitans, according to Appiah, because "many anthropologists mistrust talk about universal morality, and spend a great deal of time urging us not to intervene in the lives of other societies."[33] I fit into this category of "many anthropologists," and I mistrust cosmopolitanism for the same reason they do—its implementation of cultural imperialism.

Appiah illustrates this vision of universal morality by the following: the Indian who informs the British officer that it is Indian custom to practice suttee is informed in turn that it is the custom of the British to execute those who practice suttee. On that account, the question is not asked at all why the British have a right to be in India deciding what customs are to be executed—or, rather, who is to be executed. Speaking for myself, while I have the deepest antipathy toward suttee, I have no sympathy for colonial judicial murder, either.

Appiah, moreover, expects all of "us" (that is, the "you" he addresses explicitly in his book) to find the concept of "taboo" virtually unintelligible: "There are acts we avoid that we rather loosely call 'taboo,' of course: the prohibition on incest for example. But you don't really think incest is to be avoided because it is taboo. Your thought is exactly the other way round: it is 'taboo' because there are good reasons not to do it."[34] As a Jew—that is, one who doesn't eat any leaven for one week a year, never eats pork (even thoroughly cooked) but happily eats beef if it be slaughtered in a certain way, and who refuses to wear clothes of linen and wool together—I find it very easy to understand a taboo against eating red peppers on Wednesdays, an example of Asante practices given by Appiah, and for me, as well, the taboo on certain sexual practices is just that, a taboo and nothing more or less.[35] Appiah seems to be promulgating a practice of sympathetic understanding of other "tribes" than "ours," but the air of superiority is never absent from his discourse. For Appiah, in the end, despite his sympathetic understanding of his father's taboos, the recognition of others entails the entropy of such "local customs": "The step from 'what we don't do' to 'what we *happen* not to do' can be a small one; and then people can come to think of these practices as the sort of quaint local custom that one observes without much enthusiasm and, in the end, only when it doesn't cause too much fuss." To be sure, Appiah doesn't explicitly praise such developments; he simply seems to assume their inevitability and to treat them as "a kind of progress."[36] Bruce Robbins has observed of such cosmopolitanism: "If the neo-conservatives have been quick to attack the emergent or perhaps already dominant sensibility which supports multicultural inclusiveness, they have kept the term cosmopolitanism for themselves. Contrasting it to particularism or 'cultural egocentricity,' Dinesh D'Souza's *Illiberal Education*, for example, cites it with full approval."[37] I certainly do not mean to insinuate that Appiah is a neocon, quite the contrary, but it seems for this sort of cosmopolitanism there is not much difference between neocon and neoliberal.

I thus reject cosmopolitanism, at least of this classic variety, because of its strong tendency to impose its own colonialist, individualist, neoliberal ethics on all the peoples and people of the world. How about a great deal of enthusiasm and a sense of deep connection to ancestors, to the past, and through these to others in the present? It is precisely attitudes like Appiah's that are rendering traditional Jewish life increasingly impossible in Europe, since many Jews—not only Orthodox—hang onto those "quaint local customs" such as circumcision that violate so-called universal morality as vaunted by Appiah. If this be cosmopolitanism, I want no part of it. "Universals" that are not given life by deep appreciation of all the rich particulars to which Martiniquan poet and politician Aimé Césaire is so sensitive always simply arrogate as universal the values, beliefs, and taboos of whatever society happens to be dominant. As Césaire wrote so beautifully: "I'm not going to confine myself to some narrow particularism. But I do not intend either to become lost in a disembodied universalism. . . . I have a different idea of a universal. It is a universal rich with all that is particular, rich with all the particulars there are, the deepening of each particular, the coexistence of them all."[38] Worlds apart from Appiah.

Ultimately, then, my objection is not to the argument that Appiah makes for interaction and mutual learning as a modality for approaching moral difference, but his evident lack of concern for the deep and fruitful value of all those rich particulars. In the end his argument, it seems, comes down to some version of tolerance, not to mention (in a kind of self-contradiction) a suggestion that greater knowledge of the other provides greater odds for living together harmoniously.[39] Appiah suggests that those of us noncosmopolites who value cultural continuity (not preservation, but creative and vital continuity) are either trying to force folks to behave in certain ways and not others or, if not force, in any case to turn back the clocks. (For him, cultural continuity consists of boys wearing "traditional garb" on ceremonial occasions.) My advocacy seeks, rather, to imagine conditions and possibilities for those collectives who desire to maintain and develop traditional cultures—languages threatened by the global hegemony of English; "doings" of folks that are not conceived of as varieties of Protestant "faiths" and therefore somehow less legitimate—in a world of others. (If I am caricaturing to an extent Appiah's views, it may be owing to his habit of caricaturing the view of those he opposes, for example, claiming, as he does, that "cultural preservationists" argue for "an ideal of cultural purity" of self-contained and unchanging forms of life.)[40]

As Bruce Robbins has written, "For better or worse, there is a growing consensus that cosmopolitanism sometimes works together with nationalism rather than in opposition to it. It is thus less clear what cosmopolitanism *is* opposed to, or what its value is supposed to be."[41] It does seem as if—to use a tired cliché that seems apt here—the devil is in the details, so, as briefly as possible, here are some details. My hope is that the "world" that I here imagine will be some contribution "for better."

On my view, the absolutely crucial first step in thinking our way toward imagining such a world will be a thorough reimagining of the idea of the nation, a reimagining that, as I hope to show, now has good historical grounds. We must sever, I argue, the nation from the mononational state with which it has become so thoroughly conflated, but only, as we shall see, in quite recent times. There can be nations without states, and, moreover, states without nations—or rather with multiple nations.

In a now-classic review essay on Edward Said's *Orientalism*, James Clifford pointed out to what extent that "old idea of cosmopolitanism" inhabited his work: "It is a general feature of humanist common denominators that they are meaningless, since they bypass the local cultural codes which make personal experience possible. Said's resort to such notions underlines the absence in his book of any developed theory of culture as a differentiating and expressive ensemble rather than as simply hegemonic and disciplinary. His basic values are cosmopolitan."[42]

Clifford is subtly but decidedly against this mode of cosmopolitanism, pointing out its connections with certain modes of imagining the human individual as well as the arrogance of its ultimately Eurocentric position of superiority. "Said himself has recourse to humanist cosmopolitanism and conceptions of personal integrity, as well as to a notion of authentic development alternately glossed as 'narrative' or as a vaguely Marxist 'history.' "[43] To put this in my words, the crucial point here is that even Said has taken on the notion of the human as an individual without history or connection, a notion that is most characteristic of early modern and modern German (and from there to everywhere) thought, as social theorist Carol Breckenridge has put it sharply, indicating that we "should not conceal the fact that neoliberal cosmopolitan thought is founded on a conformist sense of what it means to be a 'person' as an abstract unity of cultural exchange."[44] In contrast, for many—if not most—of the peoples of the world, the person is imagined as already born into a web of connections and associations with people past, people present, and even a future or set of possible futures.

Clifford makes a point that I take to be vitally important: "There is no need to discard theoretically all conceptions of 'cultural' difference, especially once this is no longer seen as simply received from tradition, language or environment, but as also *made* in new political/cultural conditions of global relationality." He adds, and I cheer: "But however the culture concept is finally transcended, it should, I think, be replaced by some set of relations which preserves the concept's differential and relativist functions, and which avoids the positing of cosmopolitan essences and human common denominators."[45]

It could, perhaps fairly, be charged of me (and has been, with reference to earlier iterations of this writing) that I have chosen a soft target here. This "old ideal" of cosmopolitanism has itself been superseded in the last decades. There are, of course, subtler and more nuanced versions of cosmopolitanism than Appiah's: indeed, versions that come very close to the model of relations between cultural collectives advanced in this manifesto. Notable is the discussion by Bruce Robbins in which he suggests that it is desirable to value cosmopolitanism's "negative relation to nationality . . . without giving up an insistence on belonging—an insistence that includes the possibility of presence in other places, dispersed but real forms of membership, a density of overlapping allegiances rather than the abstract emptiness of non-allegiance."[46] Following Robbins, but with a difference, I seek to elaborate here the insistence on belonging, especially the density of overlapping allegiances, but incorporating as well a positive relation to nationality as one of those overlaps.

Robbins remarks, "It is frightening to think how little progress has been made in turning invisibly determining and often exploitative connections into conscious and self-critical ones, how far we remain from mastering the sorts of allegiance, ethics, and action that might go with our complex and multiple belonging. But this is work that has to be done."[47] Theorizing "our complex and multiple belonging" seems to me the crux of the matter. Indeed, one version of such imagining is the entire project of this book.

1

Just-So Stories: How the Diaspora Came to Be

I begin this project of political imagination by telling a brief story about the origins of the Diaspora and its alleged antidote, the State of Israel. In a sense, this is a narrative about how—under horrendous circumstances, to be sure—a nation, as I will deem it, the Jews, or Jewry, if you like, lost its way, then offer a hand-drawn map for a hardscrabble road back. I contrast my story with the standard, triumphal way that this history is generally told now.[1] Both revolve around the nature and meaning of diaspora and how it relates to concepts of nationhood.

Journalist Becky Cooper has recently written, "There are no true stories; there are only facts, and the stories we tell ourselves about those facts."[2] Any historical story is a construction, a hypothesis built up from known facts, put together by historians because they judge that this version of the story explains more of the known facts than others. Such stories also—and this is no longer a secret—lead to different judgments about the present and even the future, and the historian for multiple reasons may prefer one outcome over another. But the story told must account for the established and given facts and ideally do so better than other stories. I hope that this is what I will achieve here.

The Just-So Story till Now

The standard story goes like this. Jews were once a people like any other, with a king, a kingdom, warriors, and all of the other accoutrements of other nations, including their own religion. At a certain point, their kingdom was conquered by an empire; the Babylonians exiled much of the population to their land, where they were in effect lost (the ten tribes). After a while, the remaining Jews returned from Babylonia and set up their polity again until it, too, was conquered by yet another empire (the Romans), and the rest of the Jews were exiled from their land, but miraculously not lost. For some two millennia, give or take, Jews had been oppressed, stateless folk wandering around amid all of the other, proper nations that had their own lands and states until one of those proper nations decided to solve the problem of all of those Jews who didn't fit in anywhere by exterminating them. That nation didn't quite manage the feat, and a lot of the wandering Jews came back to the ancestral ethnostate, where, after defeating their enemies, they built a new nation-state just for Jews, a triumphal and final restoration of the correct state of the Jews.

In this account, the conception of a "diaspora" appears in two ways. The first is chronological and refers to an earlier past in which the nation was one and sovereign, a condition that was interrupted, leaving it homeless, weak, and assailable. The second is spatial, offering a descriptive model in which there is now a situation of homeland versus diaspora.[3] Homeland, once again, is imagined as ideal, diaspora as deeply, profoundly, necessarily a defective condition.

A New Just-So Story

Here is my revisionist version of the story (not only mine, of course). In antiquity, the ancestors of the people we call Jews were more or less like any other folk of their time in terms of their social structures. They dwelt in a particular stretch of land, although it wasn't a country, for countries hadn't been invented yet, had a king (or, frequently enough, two rival kings), their own cult(s), language, and various forms of an epic telling the story of where they came from. They were frequently allied with or dominated by one or another of the great empires of the ancient Near East, the Egyptian or Mesopotamian.

So far, my story more or less tracks the first version. My version parts ways with the standard Jewish narrative somewhat later, however, sometime during the Hellenistic and Roman periods. During this period, people from Judea, the people we will later call "Jews" (*Juifs* in French, *Juden* in German, *Iddin* in Yiddish, *Yehudim* in Hebrew) scattered—voluntarily, for the most part—into different places in the Hellenistic, Greek-speaking world and made homes there. In places such as Alexandria and many others, they lived according to Judean customs, worshipped the Judean god, read the Torah in a Greek translation, and produced some highly significant Jewish literature in Greek, such as the works of Philo and the *Wisdom of Solomon*.[4] They referred to themselves by the Greek word *diaspora*. Diaspora, for them, felt more like establishing Judean colonies than anything else.

Despite many desperate travails over the centuries, the Jewish nation persisted and created culture of all kinds, in substantial part owing to the productive interaction with other cultures in their environments, and those interactions were then transmitted to other Jews elsewhere as well.

Diaspora or Exile?

Since even quite a bit before the destruction of the Jewish polity in Palestine, Jews have lived in, even created colonies in, many places, at first within the Mediterranean world and then farther afield. In our present day, there is a strong tendency to identify "diaspora" with exile, a concept central to the standard account, especially with respect to Jews. In the Alexandrian Greek translation of the Bible known as the Septuagint, from the third century B.C., however, the Greek word *diaspora* is almost never used to translate words that mean exile. Instead, it uses a mixture of both positive and negative terms, such as *sojourning, captivity,* or *colony.* "Diaspora," in its ancient Greek sense, while founded on a word meaning "scattering," most frequently focuses more on the creation of new homes, not on being absent from a home, for which they generally use the word *apoikia* (literally, away from home).[5] When referring to themselves, the Alexandrian Jews use "diaspora," not the words they use to translate the biblical "exile." In other words, exile was something different from diaspora; they were not exiles, an unhappy condition, but in diaspora, and not at all unhappy at that.[6] Philo, the great Jewish-Alexandrian philosopher of the first century, regarded the Judeans as a people on the same level as Romans or early Greeks and referred to the Jewish Diaspora "as rather a positive colonization: the colonies abroad . . . in other prosperous lands preserve the customs of the mother-city."[7] If we read "customs" here as all of the elements of a Jewish form of life, then we are close to the imagining of diaspora suggested in this manifesto.

In Hebrew/Aramaic, even the term *galut* (quite literally "exile") is not always negatively charged. Thus, the Rabbis of the Mishna can say: "Be a *goleh* [that is, exile yourself!] to a place of Torah!" These Rabbis, living in the Holy Land, advise the Jewish man [!] to leave even Palestine when it is barren of Torah and travel to live in a place where Torah is studied and created even outside of the Land of Israel. Exile is configured here as a positive space and given a positive valuation.

Indeed, that is how the Rabbis of the Talmud themselves frequently understood the move to Babylonia: not as a disaster, but as a move to a better place, where the Torah could be studied more easily.[8] We cannot think of the Jewish Diaspora, therefore, as always and everywhere being understood as a forced and oppressive exile. Today, "diaspora" may suggest dislocation and possibly distress, but it was not always so; in the future, we might again think of the settlements of Jews not in their putative land, the Diaspora, as enhancing, developing the customs, in the broadest sense, of the Jewish nation. Both for the Greek-speaking Jews of the Hellenistic world and for the Semitic speakers of Babylonia, at any rate, diaspora was not understood as a negative or even anomalous condition for the Jews to abide within, but one full of creative possibilities.

Since I've written extensively on this topic already, two pithy examples here will have to do for making this point concrete. First, in direct contradiction to current neo-Zionist ideology, the Talmud claims that Jews are safer when they are scattered in at least two places than when they are all gathered together. As the Talmud [Pesachim 87b] relates:

> Rabbi ʿOshaya said: What is it that is written "even the Righteous acts toward the inhabitants of his villages [*pirzono*] in Israel (Judges 5:11). *The Holy Blessed One acted righteously toward Israel by scattering* [pizrono] *them among the nations* [emphasis added]. And this is identical to what a certain sectarian [*min*] said to Rabbi Yehuda Nesia: "We are superior to you, for it says of you: 'For six months did Joab remain there with all Israel, until he had cut off every male in Edom' (1 Kings 11:16), but you have been among us for many years and we haven't done anything to you."[9] He said to him [the sectarian]: "If you will, one of the students will answer you." Rabbi ʿOshaya answered him: "That's because you didn't know what to do. If you wanted to kill all of us, . . . [you couldn't because] we're not all among you, and if you killed those who are among you, they would call you a cutting-off kingdom!"

[That would precisely deprive you of your point of pride!] He said to him, "By the Agape of Rome [Isis!], that's what we think about when we get up and when we lie down."[10]

In contrast to the standard (Zionist) story, the Jewish People in this text are less vulnerable, safer, when distributed between two empires or among even more different sovereignties, because no one evil emperor can endeavor to kill us all. Ahashverus could, according to the book of Esther, because he allegedly ruled all 129 nations from the Ganges to Kush. It took a very wise woman to save us from that (fictional) threat, but according to the Talmud, G-d's plan of scattering us between powers renders it impossible for one of them to completely commit genocide upon us.

The sense of the positive virtues of diaspora goes even further, however, for according to other passages in the Talmud, not only is Babylonian Diaspora a mode of safekeeping for the Jews, but also a place in which Torah study and creativity is enhanced. Why, asks the Talmud, has G-d sent the Jews to Babylonia?

> Rabbi Ḥanina says, "It is because their language [Aramaic] is close to the language of Torah [and therefore good for the study thereof]." Rabbi Yoḥanan says, "Because he sent them to the House of their Mother. Its exemplum is of a man who becomes angry at his wife, to where does he send her? To the house of her mother." 'Ulla said, "It was in order that they will eat dates and be busy with Torah."

Not only is the great advantage of Babylonia that their Semitic speech, which is close to the Hebrew of Torah, promotes the study of Torah, according to the first speaker, but the Palestinian Rabbi Yoḥanan turns the "exile" in Babylon into a homecoming to their motherland, the land, after all, from which Abraham is commanded to "go forth from *your* land to the land that I will show you!"[11] The entire notion of diaspora as the act of forced dispersion from a single homeland is exploded by the Talmud at this moment, and by a Palestinian speaker, nay, the leader of the Palestinian Rabbis in his day—if, of course, the attribution is to be trusted. Indeed, as Isaiah Gafni points out, this statement reads almost as if it is an "embracing of what is usually considered a uniquely Hellenistic idea, namely that Israel, like other ethnic groups, have a dual homeland (δευτέρα πατρίς)." Babylonia is portrayed here not only as a second homeland but as the original homeland from which the Jews have come to Palestine. The concepts of homeland and Holy Land are thus, at least for these Rabbis, not coterminous.[12] Far from being sent into an oppressive situation, the Jews were brought to a refuge in the place in which they would feel most at home, returning home, as it were, owing to their ancient roots and cultural ties with that place.[13]

There is, to be sure, ambivalence signified here as well. Even though Babylonia is pictured repeatedly as a place of refuge, nonetheless, there *is* a sense of exile from the Holy Land that also is encoded. A bride being sent to her mother's house is, of course, the sign of the at least temporary dissolution of a marriage. This does not mean, then, that the Jews abandoned the ancient hope to be restored to the Holy Land, but as so poignantly evoked, especially by Jewish liturgy, this was an apocalyptic hope, for the end of times, for the whole world, and not a structuring principle for life in the here and now. For now, despite having been exiled from the husband's house, we are at home in the mother's safe refuge and warm embrace.

Seen in this light, diaspora was not an interruption of the history of the Jews but an essential moment in that history; indeed, it became the condition of Jewish life for centuries thereafter. To be sure, the Jews frequently suffered and suffered dearly during many of those times and in many of those places, but they also thrived and created, with the Talmud as the living center of shared existence over time and space.[14] Much of that creativity and vitality was the product of the fruitful miscegenation, as it were, of shared Jewish culture all over the world with the local and vibrantly different cultures of the lands in which Jews ended up.[15] Not at all at a loss for home, Jews made a home in diaspora, as a scattered, but deeply conjoined folk.

The reclamation of the Diaspora Nation involves attending to its foundational import as a defining character of Jewish existence, as well as to its cultural and political vitality.[16] Conceiving of diaspora as an entirely negative condition has provided the underpinnings for the neo-Zionist mode of thinking known as "negation of the diaspora" (שלילת הגלות), the idea, especially promulgated by David Ben-Gurion (and after him by a host of others), that not only must there be a sovereign state of the Jews, a Jewish state, but that all Jews ideally would move there and thus the diaspora, as an anomalous and tragic situation, would be eliminated.[17] In Ben-Gurion's view, all Jews who didn't join the Zionist project in Palestine were simply waste products, "dust," or even soap (common Israeli usage about refugee Jews after the war, not Ben-Gurion's). This view persists even today. For Natan Sharansky and many other Jewish voices, all Jews who do not join the territorialist nationalist project of the State of Israel are simply "un-Jews," whatever their commitment to Jewish learning or practice.[18] The Nazis, of course, offered a terrible Final Solution to the Jewish problem, Ben-Gurion an only less terrible vision: a final solution to the Diaspora. Those who find this formulation too extreme may not be aware that Ben-Gurion explicitly wrote (in a letter) that it was better that half the Jews of Europe die in the Nazi genocide if the other half would come to Palestine, rather than have them all survive and remain outside of the Jewish state.

Other Zionist views—nearly totally occluded by now—included versions of the multinational state proposed by Leon Pinsker (discussed at some length below), Judah Magnes, and others. However, Zionism now fit—and must needs fit—into what historian Noam Pianko names "the sovereign mold," in which territorial boundaries are in direct correlation with the dwelling of particular national populations; each national group has a right of self-determination, defined as the right to political independence somewhere for that group alone, and all substate loyalties must be subsumed to loyalty to that nation-state. This set of ideas was renamed "Zionism," in the case of the Jews, and afterward quite quickly became the only legitimate referent for the term.[19] The ideational and perhaps even practical payoff of demonstrating the very recent and deeply contested (even among Zionists) nature of the allegedly irrevocable nexus between nation and state is to make more plausible the claim that something put together can be once more revoked.

Rejecting neo-Zionist ideas of diaspora as an anomalous, if not pathological, condition, with Jews perhaps its only example and the state its only cure, I propose diaspora as a kind of cultural situation in which a group of people—the Jews, for instance—are doubly situated (culturally) at home and abroad, located in their *doikayt*—here and now—but also culturally and affectively bound to similar collectives that are in other places, and perhaps other times as well, which we could name their *Yiddishkayt*, their Jewishness, or, in order to avoid Ashkenazocentrism, their *Judezmo* or *Judaïté*. Any future for the Jewish People will necessitate an inclusion of all of the Jews and cannot include only European or Eurocentric terms.[20]

Israeli historian and political theorist Amnon Raz-Krakotzkin writes of his concept of exile: "As a cultural position, it grants meaning and value to a heterogeneous reality by turning toward the foundations repressed by the concept of negation of exile; moreover, it also recognizes the existence and rights of the Palestinian collective and its viewpoint. In the concept of exile is thus embodied a consistent moral position, on which critique can be grounded."[21]

I agree, but there is a difference between us, too. Both of us propose that the situation of the Jews without sovereignty holds significant promise, but while Raz-Krakotzkin defines that promise under the figure of exile and produces an account of morality out of it, I am thinking in terms of diaspora, not exile, and looking for a just political solution—just to all forms of life (*Lebensformen*).[22] I am not suggesting that these approaches are incompatible with each other; I suggest, rather, that they add to or supplement each other. We both imagine a binational state in Palestine; the question is how we get there—conceptually. I call for a diasporic state of (at least) two nations in Palestine. The model of diaspora that I adumbrate throughout this manifesto, if it doesn't quite provide solutions, perhaps provides some terms within which to imagine future systems of thought and structures that recall aspects of the past.

I have elsewhere imagined and advanced this new-old usage for the word *diaspora,* and it is by using these terms that I am proposing an old-new mode of Jewish existence.[23] The first term, *doikayt*, is drawn from the language of the Jewish Bund, the Yiddish socialist mass movement of pre–World War II Jews in Central and Eastern Europe. It translates quite literally as "hereness," which I'm adopting as my term for the commitment to the welfare of the people among whom I—we—live. It involves primarily class solidarity, but can very easily be extended to the struggle for justice for all oppressed in my city, state, country. The second term, *Yiddishkayt* or *Judaïté*, signifies the national ties and commitments to other collectives that I identify as part of my nation even when living under other political formations or states, the people with whom I share a history and other stories, songs, foods, holidays, modes of speech—and humor as well as memories of horrific suffering. By writing *Yiddishkayt/Judaïté*, I am explicitly indicating my intention to expand the nation beyond the Eastern and Central European realm of the Ashkenazi, Yiddish-speaking Jews encompassed by the Bund, via a terminological move to include all of the tribes of Israel, speakers of Yiddish, *Judezmo*, Judeo-Aramaic, Judeo-Persian, Greek, and a multitude of others. The Jews, whatever they are, are not a European ethnicity. The Bund's perspective gives us the model to move beyond it, a prospect for which I will argue in the ensuing chapters of this manifesto.

2

Bad Faith: Why the Jews Aren't a Religion

Until quite recently, it has commonly been held that every human group has a "religion." It has been notoriously difficult to define the word "religion" and thus to delineate the concept, although myriad attempts have been made. Notwithstanding this stumbling block, it seems fair to say that in modern usage, we have had a pretty good idea what we mean when we call something a religion, even without being in absolute agreement what is in and what is out of the category.[1] At the same time, however, it is increasingly recognized that the concept of "religion" as an autonomous sphere of human activity, separate or separable from other spheres of activity named as the realm of the secular, such as law, politics, kinship, and economics, is itself as modern (and as "Western") as is the usage of the word "religion" to denote that sphere.[2] Because, as is now recognized by many scholars, "religion" as a concept and category emerged out of the very forces that defined it, during the time of the Enlightenment, it becomes very difficult to imagine how a Jewish religion could possibly exist as such before any religion did—that is, before one aspect of the things humans do is separated out, isolated from cultural activity in general, and named, however it is defined, "religion." "Judaism" as a "religion," as the term is commonly understood today, emerged only as a product of modernity.[3] This point can be sharpened even further, for the forces that historically produced the category of "religion" as a distinct entity from the "secular" during the seventeenth century in

Europe are precisely the same forces that raised the "Jewish Question" to the center of attention—a position that in one way or another it has occupied since then.[4] As political theorist and postcolonial writer Aamir Mufti has pointed out, the "projects of secularism," citizenship, separation of church and state, national language, national literature and culture, "have circled around the question of the Jews."[5] Just to cite one example: the question of how French (or Russian) one had to be in order to be included into the polity of the French or Russian state was first confronted and debated with reference to the Jews, or, as Aimé Césaire once put it, Europe tried out on the Jews what it would later practice in the colonies.

There was no separate Jewish faith; there were Jewish beliefs, Jewish practices (not all of them liturgical or mandated by the Torah)—all of life was Jewish doings. There was no separate "religion" at all.

So that was then, but what about now?[6] Aren't the Jews a religion now?[7] Not in any normative or prescriptive sense. There are myriad Jews, myriads of myriads of Jews, who do not profess any religion and yet are deeply engaged with the Jewish mystery, Jews producing literature and other culture in Jewish idioms, whether in Hebrew or in Yiddish or in both and in other Jewish languages as well. Sigmund Freud provides an explicit and excellent example, writing that he was free of religion, a "godless Jew," but "very much a Jew."[8] And such folks are recognized as Jews by other Jews. Manifestly, one does not have to be a part of a religion in order to be Jewish.

The distinguished American political theorist Michael Walzer of the Institute for Advanced Studies in Princeton, in a strenuous defense of Zionism, demonstrates appositely the fallacy involved in any argument supporting anti-Zionism based on the claim that "Judaism" is a religion and that the idea of a Jewish People a fictional—or even fraudulent—way of claiming national status for an alleged scattering of religious congregations around the world.[9] Walzer notes that the

Jews share many characteristics of a nationality, a national group, or even a nation, even (or especially) in Ernest Renan's sense that the "essence of a nation is that all individuals have many things in common, and also that they have forgotten many things."[10] This compelling argument is, in essence, Walzer's reason for denying that the Jews constitute a religion.

Here's a second reason why it's not a good idea to exchange the historical visions of the Jews as a nation for a claim that they are a church. If the Jews wish to take advantage of laws that depend on Christian definitions of "religion," which are essentially all the definitions there are, we will end up with a "Judaism" that looks very much like Christianity, that is, belonging defined by belief, "the Jewish faith," "*jüdische Glaube*," something we might call—with no offense intended—Jewtheranism.[11] As Gil Anidjar has remarked, wittily summing up Edward Said's thinking, "*Wo es war*—where Christianity was, there is now religion."[12] "Religion" is Christian, and if a so-called Judaism is a religion, then it is a variant form of Christianity (a "heresy"): if you believe this way, you are a Christian, and if you believe that way, you are a Jew.

These beliefs, moreover, are normatively of no interest whatever to the public sphere. As Aamir Mufti has concisely stated, "This is the Jewish emancipation that liberalism promises from its very inception. Enlightenment . . . thus requires the privatization of religious affiliation, that is, its confinement to the (patriarchal) realm of the (bourgeois) family under the rubric of practice and belief. The signs of religious affiliation and community must cease to have a public existence."[13] In other words, the price of so-called Jewish emancipation is the destruction of Jewish community and culture in favor of a confinement of Jewishness to sorts of sentiments and even practices that characterize Protestantism—even though the sentiments and practices are not identical, of course: you go to church on Sunday; we go to synagogue on Saturday. You believe in the Trinity; we don't believe thus. No wonder Kant observed that *Judentum* is not a religion; in his day, it was very, very different from Lutheranism—still. One reason that certain versions of a "religion" named *Judentum* have been so successful in postwar Germany is precisely that they look exactly like Protestantism from a broadly cultural point of view, thus eliminating effectively the *Judaïté* that incorporates way more than *Glaube* (faith), the modes of eating, dressing, melodies of speech, attitudes toward sex, and more that constitute all of Jewish culture.[14] And Max Weinreich pointed out with reference to an earlier scholar's identification of "religion," *Judaïté* (*Yiddishkayt*) is what joins Jews the world over: "Today many Jews and Christians live in essentially the same fashion, and the difference all year is merely that [the] former attend (or can attend) services on Saturday and the latter on Sunday. In relation to the rise of language, one should not speak of the Jewish religion, but of Jewishness [*Yiddishkeit* (*sic*)]. In the traditional Jewishness of diverse culture areas there are many variants and even contradictions; and yet Jewishness has linked all Jews over time and space in a community of historical fate and in a consciousness of this fate."[15]

In former times, Jews were a whole (by this I don't mean simplex) culture-nation, speaking their own way, worshipping their own way, dressing, eating, marrying, rearing children their own ways. All of this and more was deeply informed by the Talmud, not just the worship and all of its appliances, but all of it, and all of it imbricated and intertwined. It is impossible to pull one thread and say this is the "religion" of the Jews without the entire fabric unraveling and disintegrating.

Franz Rosenzweig seems to have understood this clearly, writing to Gerhard (Gershom) Scholem in the context of the usage of such words as *Judentum* and *Jüdische Glaube* (the Jewish faith) to refer to ourselves: "In a sense we are ourselves guests at our own table, we ourselves, I myself. So long as we speak German (or even if we speak

Hebrew, modern Hebrew, the Hebrew of '1921') we cannot avoid this detour that again and again leads us the hard way from what is alien back to our own."[16] In the past, in the Hebrew of before 1921, and in Yiddish, such usages are not to be found, and by using them, we take on ourselves a character "not ours."

"Freedom of Religion" and the Offense of Circumcision

The result of defining something called "Judaism" as a religion, something "not ours," is seemingly a grotesque mismatch in which the Christian "faith" always comes out on top.[17] Legal scholars Lena Salaymeh (Oxford and EHESS, Paris) and Shai Lavi (Tel Aviv University Law School and Van Leer Institute) explicate how the assignment of "religion" to a separate and defined sphere, and especially its internalization, is what clears out the space of the secular, remarking acutely as well that "late antique Christian criticisms of Judaism linger in the state's construction of religion."[18] What renders such secular clearing and construction of religion Christian, and perhaps especially Protestant, is the focus on the individual and his or her "faith," his or her ostensibly free choice to be saved through belief or not.[19] This privatization of "religion," taking it out of the public (or at any rate, the political) sphere, empowers discourses on the model of being a Jew at home and a German in public, to give one example.

What makes Salaymeh and Lavi's essay particularly relevant here is its specific application to the fraught issue of circumcision. We can see from their discussion how defining "Judaism" as a religion and its incorporation into a Lutheran concept of religion as faith or belief system, as opposed to corporate belonging, wreaks havoc with Jewish and Islamic self-understandings. For example: a German court quite recently wanted to ban infant circumcision as a violation of the child's "self-determination," that is, his religious freedom. By circumcising the child, he is allegedly prevented from choosing to be or to become a Christian or an unbeliever when he grows up.[20] Salaymeh and Lavi show how European state discourses about male circumcision are dependent on the production of "religion" by the secular state and the construction of circumcision as a matter of "private belief." This results in discrimination against so-called religious minorities, paradoxically "under the doctrine of religious freedom."[21] That is, according to the Cologne court—explicitly—the wicked Jewish parents of their male infant are allegedly depriving this monad individual of his freedom to choose freely to believe in the Incarnation and Resurrection because, after all, this poor child has been circumcised—as Jesus and Paul both were.

The result in the United States is what Will Herberg defined decades ago as the three forms of American Protestantism: Catholic Protestantism, Protestant Protestantism, and Jewish Protestantism. (By now, we should add Muslim and Buddhist Protestantism—or maybe not). My issue here is not, of course, with Protestantism itself, but in the way that, as amply shown by scholars, it ends up defining "religion" and thus "religious freedom" on the model of Protestantism, which places individual private faith and "salvation" over corporate identity and places inner movements of the psyche over communal practices or "doings." As Salaymeh and Lavi point out, when this becomes the publicly promulgated version of "religion," it is inherently discriminatory vis-à-vis Jews and Muslims, as opposed to Christians. They remark: "We propose that the implications of understanding religion as individual belief differ for Muslims and Jews, as compared to Christians. Although secular law elevates a definition of religion as individual belief, it also recognizes religion as practice, but primarily when that practice is evident in positive law. Likewise, secular law privileges a definition of religion as individual, but also recognizes religion as communal (or collective) when it marks particular groups as a public threat."

The Cologne court is imagining the human subject as a monad with no history and completely autonomous in defining their identity, "beliefs," practices, and affiliations, while the Jews stand precisely against such notions of the "self." We Jews purvey the sources of the nonself of the person, who is already, without willing, thrown or inscribed into a bond with others not of their own "free" choice.[22] In other words, the Cologne court, like all colonial powers, is making judgments on the basis of theological/philosophical bases that it claims are universal, but are in fact highly culturally specific. Thinking of Jewry as being a "religion" inevitably involves the imposition—even the willing imposition—of the West on a people not of the West, however much in it.[23] As in the case of cosmopolitanism discussed above, high ideals are shown by this to be colonial impositions of power in disguise.

Thus, when Jews claim that Judaism is a religion, we're inevitably falling into a trap, since religion is understood quite differently than Jewish belonging. We ought no longer to reject Immanuel Kant's notorious observation that "Judaism is really not a religion at all but merely a union of a number of people who, because they belonged to a single stock, formed themselves into a commonwealth under purely political laws, and not into a church."[24] The rejection of "faith" is precisely signified, as Kant understood well, in the preconscious marking of the penis; the sign is only for men, of course, but the demand is to men and women alike. (This is meant as a descriptive, not normative nor apologetic, claim on my part.) A testimony: in a 1795 letter to the writer David Veit, Berlin salon Jewess (*sic*) Rahel Varnhagen confessed that she imagined that at her birth "some supramundane being . . . plunged these words with a dagger into my heart: 'Yes, have sensibility, see the world as few see it, be great and noble, nor can I deprive you of restless, incessant thought. But with one reservation: Be a Jewess!' " She goes on to say, "Now, my life is one long bleeding" and declares defiantly, "I shall never accept that I am a schlemiel and a Jewess." A dagger in the heart; a knife to the penis. The claim of Jewishness is also a theoretical and rhetorical claim, a command to any child: "Be a Jew!"

Varnhagen's confession is a perfect example of the experience of interpellation, "the process by which ideology, embodied in major social and political institutions . . . constitutes the very nature of individual subjects' identities through the process of 'hailing' them in social interactions." Varnhagen was unhappy with this constitution of her subjectivity as a "Jew" against her will; here, of course, one might claim that gender is one possible differentiating factor, although by no means an ineluctable one, even in earlier modern Europe.[25] I repeat that I am not making here a feminist point or an apology for anything. This being thrown, as it were, into the world as a Jew, called at birth, is experienced differently, obviously, by different individuals and even classes of individuals, especially, in this circumstance, different genders, but it has its power. Even when we reject, later on—and we are free to do so—the tradition into which we are born, that rejection shapes us as well. Only the powerful symbolic marker of that existential givenness, the mark of the covenant, remains to remind us that Jewishness for men and for women is not chosen. We are thrown into the world Jews, to make of that what we will. It is this thrownness or interpellation that the Cologne court wishes to cancel.

With the entry into the modern, "enlightened" world, there is an entrance fee, a fairly steep one. As W. J. T. Mitchell once remarked wittily in another context: "There is no representation without taxation." This movement into modernity constitutes a total paradigm shift in German Jewish self-consciousness, a shift that extended itself ultimately far beyond German lands. It is owing to the shock waves released by that earthquake that in the present, by and large, there is the nearly perfect binary and mutually exclusive opposition in conceptions of what "the Jews" denotes, a religion or a nation/ethnicity, with seemingly no other options.[26]

The danger of even buying into the binary opposition of religion/nation is palpable, whichever choice we make. Another court case in a Western European court makes this clear. The British Supreme Court in 2009 decided a case against an Orthodox Jewish school that, allowed to discriminate by religion under British law, rejected a boy who, though allegedly devout, did not have a Jewish mother. The court's reasoning is as illuminating as that of the Cologne court: "One thing is clear about the matrilinear test; it is a test of ethnic origin," Lord Phillips, president of the court, said in his majority opinion. Under the law, he said, "by definition, discrimination that is based upon that test, is discrimination on racial grounds."[27] Note several things about this opinion: first of all, it conflates ethnicity with race, and second, it ignores the fact that the child could simply have undergone a conversion ceremony. One cannot normally convert into a "race," suggesting at the very least that the English judge was not thinking very deeply or subtly. I have also never heard of racial determination based on whether or not a progenitor was male or female. It is at least possible—and I will argue so—that whatever it is that constitutes Jewish genealogy, it is not identical to race.

Moreover, the religious bias involved in the court's ruling becomes totally clear in a further statement about the opinion: "The ruling represents a definitive end to six decades of exclusion of children who are devout in their Jewish faith, but considered by some to be not Jewish enough to enjoy the benefits of their community's leading faith school, [according to] John Halford, a lawyer for M [the child]."[28] Notwithstanding the fact that some millennium and a half of the definition of Jewishness via the mother and not six decades of some clerical prejudice lie behind the school's policy, this quotation is very telling. For Jews, at least for some, faith (by which is meant assent to certain propositions) is required of Jews, but in no opinions rendered by traditional Jewish authorities is it determinative of who is a Jew and who isn't. Jews are always going to be in trouble when we have Protestants determining who is or who is not a Jew. We will see, however, that the racialized understanding of Jewishness is an ever-present danger that must be guarded against vigilantly.

Family, Not Race

Arguably, Franz Rosenzweig (1886–1929) was the most significant thinker to date of Jewish modernity. His thought is crucial here, because in what seems at first glance to be a notoriously racist account of Jewish collective existence, he actually provides, on careful—and con-troversial—rereading, what I take to be a way to interpret Jewish ge-nealogy in precisely a nonracist way. This reread Rosenzweigian account is thus crucial to my project here of rendering strong, vital attachment to *Judaïté* part of a progressive way of life.

In a provocative declaration that seems at first (and perhaps even second) glance to blow a staggeringly racist dog whistle, Rosenzweig, contrasting the Jew with the Christian, says: "Only he belongs to Christianity who knows his own life to be on the way which leads from Christ come to Christ coming. This knowledge is belief. It is belief as the content of a testimony. It is belief in something [*Glaube an etwas*]. That is exactly the opposite of the belief of the Jew. His belief is not the content of a testimony, but rather the product of a reproduction. The Jew, engendered a Jew, attests his belief by con-tinuing to procreate the Jewish people. His belief is not in something: he is himself the belief."[29]

This claim has been interpreted as a bare confession of "racial" superiority. (One recent reader even interpreted it to mean that "the Jew" is meant to worship himself.) But not only is Rosenzweig's claim here not a racist account, as we will see, it provides us with a way out of the terrible pitfall of Jewish supremacy and racism, which do, indeed, dog our heels. Rosenzweig stands in opposition to racism precisely because he attributes no superior character to the Jews, indeed, he attributes to them no character at all, surely nothing innate, other than the sheer existential fact of being genealogically a Jew.[30] The Jew is pure existence as a Jew; this existence is prior to any essence whatever.

What's at issue is how to signify that difference today. In the antinomies whose impasses I'm trying to suggest we should and can escape, the alternative to signifying Jewishness as a religion has seemed sometimes to be only to represent it as constituted by race. This is borne out, it would seem, by the recent actions of the Israeli rabbinate—or at any rate, some of it—in declaring folks Jews on the basis of their mitochondrial DNA. Mitochondrial DNA traces descent through the matrilineal line, as opposed to nuclear DNA, which is transmitted by both parents. Since according to normative rabbinic practice from antiquity on, Jewishness is determined by the mother, not the father, the presence of "Jewish" mitochondria is being taken—somewhat grotesquely—again, by *some* rabbis, to indicate true Jewish descent going back forever. This is, to me and to many others, a horrifying instance of biologization of a cultural conception. Since the stated reason for matrilineal descent in rabbinic tradition is that the mother raises the child most intimately, it hardly seems to attend at all to the meaning of the law to claim that someone is Jewish simply because fifteen generations ago, someone in the family was, indeed, Jewish, even if no one has known of that biological fact until now. That, indeed, would smack of racism in its grossest sense.

But is it so? Rosenzweig, I contend, shows us why not. Some rhetorical questions: Has this been the historical self-conception of the Jews—as opposed to the conception held by the Nazis, for instance?

Do practices of genealogy and endogamy (marrying "in," not "out") constitute the Jews as a race or, even more troubling, as necessarily racist? Have the Jews imagined themselves as biologically different from other peoples of the earth?

For the vastly greater part, the answer to these questions is no: racialized Jewish self-fashioning is, I think, something of an anomaly, although to my horror, less and less so. In the stories Jews tell about themselves and each other, their shared narrative, the narrative of the Jewish collective, the model for thinking about Jewish corporate existence is and has been that of family. Selah Boyarin had gotten it by the age of four:

SELAH HANNA BOYARIN: Are you Jewish, Zaidie?
ZAIDIE: Yes, I sure am.
SELAH: Because you're in the family! I'm Jewish too, because I'm in our family.

Selah had indeed grasped it. We are Jews owing to the fact that we are a family. And you don't choose your family, nor are you part of it owing to its particular character, for better or worse. And family is much, much more than a matter of some molecules in the body.

While families can and do incorporate much violence, this way of thinking of the genealogical component of the existence of the Jews is superior to racial thinking. Insistence on family intimacy and shared interest does not imply anything essentialistic about the particular family, just that it is a family, and certainly not that it is superior in essence to all other families.

The finest, most precise, and also beautiful articulation of this kind of connection has, I think, been given by legal historian Patricia Williams. It is worth an extended quotation:

I cannot help but see the bodies of my near ancestors in the current caravans of desperate souls fleeing from place to place, chased by famine, war and toxins. "The bodies of my ancestors" may sound romantic, but I take the idea seriously. I am not speaking here of biologized inheritance: my epigenetics, my predispositions for depression or resilience. Instead, I mean the inheritance of linguistically and rhetorically embedded traditions passed on in habits of speech. I am composed of the voices of those who bred me. We are talked into the world by our forebears: by how they parsed words or not. . . . Their emotional inflections and instincts for fight or flight inhabit us, inhabit me. Their accented soundscape is the familiarity through which we filter all experience. It is an idea of home, even when groundless, or unsupported by structure, or bereft of actual landscape.[31]

When I read this, I realized that these are exactly words I want to say about Jews—without claiming any particular political or moral equivalence between the black and the Jewish historical experiences, these words vocalize for me precisely that sense of intimacy that is not biologically conditioned. If I could have, I would have written these words myself; they so clearly capture what I want to say. We, too, have a collective grounded in a soundscape, a familiarity through which we filter experience (I left out the "all"). Insofar as these specific "rhetorically embedded traditions" are shared by others who equally are divested of actual landscape and do it somewhere else, we have a diaspora, a "family," of ancestors, grounded in a narrative of genealogy and not sovereignty; time and not space.[32]

3
Bad Blood: Why the Jews Aren't a Race

Consanguinity, the phenomenon of being descended from the same ancestor, shared "blood," is one of the most powerful of symbols for human connection and disconnection, motivator of extraordinary acts of self-sacrifice and kindness as well as the most extraordinary acts of cruelty, violence, and even genocide: "Ties of blood"; "Blood is thicker than water"; "Blood and soil."[1] I want to reclaim here that power for peaceful ends while at the same time tempering it with the claims of affinity—affines are the people with whom we *choose* to be in social groups (typically relatives by marriage), the opposite of consanguinity. Moreover, I wish to insist that the use of this symbol need not imply racist claims. If a black Jew is related to me by storied ties of common ancestry, then it is clear that we are not speaking of "race" in the ordinary sense when we speak of "Jewish blood," but something else. But if not race, then what?

We can answer by looking at how consanguinity has been figured in traditional Jewish texts. While common descent is a very powerful topos in the Hebrew Bible, "blood" is not generally used to denote it. This is not to deny the significance of blood as a powerful symbol, but it is not a symbol of race or even of kinship or the ties that bind and divide within the classical Hebrew concept world. Gil Anidjar has noted: "There is little room . . . to doubt that, for the Bible more than for classical Greece, blood is a symbol of life, of mere life, and indeed of the flesh."[2] Anidjar goes on to explicate that it is not the physical

nature of blood that makes it such a powerful symbol of connectedness, but its circulation: it is "the peculiar way in which blood circu-
lates" that "produces its efficacy as a symbol."[3] Blood is actually a
terrible symbol for "race" in its modern sense—of a collection of biological characteristics—since everyone (or nearly everyone) understands very well that genetics has virtually nothing to do with blood.

But more broadly, as a symbol, "blood" does not involve essences
of any kind at all. As Anidjar has argued, "Blood . . . is a word. It is
merely a name here, a figure, a metonymy," the figure of part for part.
"It is only the name we give to something else, and for some other
thing. What is that thing, then?"[4] It clearly isn't some particular characteristic feature being shared by all. Let's not forget, after all, that
"family resemblance" is Wittgenstein's name for groups that are
formed without even one particular characteristic feature. The
only thing that joins the members of a family (say, "the Jews") is
their membership itself, however that has been defined within the
collective.

Consider the following statement by Rosenzweig. Once again, at
first, it sounds grotesquely and egregiously racist:

> There is only one community in which such a linked se-
> quence of everlasting life goes from grandfather to grandson,
> only one which cannot utter the "we" of its unity without
> hearing deep within a voice that adds: "are eternal." It must
> be a blood community, because only blood gives present war-
> rant to the hope for a future. . . . Only a community based on
> common blood feels the warrant of eternity warm in its veins
> even now. . . . Among the peoples of the earth, the Jewish
> people is "the one people," as it calls itself on the high rung of
> its life, which it ascends Sabbath after Sabbath. . . . We were
> the only ones who trusted in blood and abandoned the land;

and so, we preserved the priceless sap of life which pledged us that it would be eternal. Among the peoples of the world, we were the only ones who separated what lived within us from all community with what is dead.[5]

This paragraph demands some earnest interpretation. First of all, we must attend to the catachresis in Rosenzweig's use of "blood" here, since, as I have already mentioned, this is *not* a usage found in premodern Jewish texts, which are wont to refer to "seed" or "flesh" (flesh of my flesh), or even "bone."[6] Second, we must attend to the crux whereby Rosenzweig bases the eternality of "blood" precisely and necessarily on renunciation of the land. It is only by renouncing temporal power that any claims for a particular Jewish pith can be posited at all. The intimacy of Jewish interconnection—as "thick" as that of siblings or lovers, *pace* Appiah—can be sustained ethically only in the renunciation of sovereignty over a particular piece of land.[7] Hence Rosenzweig's absolute rejection of Zionism, "abandoning the land." This is a deep ethical and ontological commitment on his part, and not a matter of political opinions so-called.

With this background, we can begin to understand the difficult passage in Rosenzweig better. Rosenzweig is saying that the substitution of genealogy for compatriotism enables a kind of eternality precisely because it enables existence without prior essence: a Jew is a Jew is a Jew, not one who believes this or does that, but simply one who is born to a certain people anywhere or has become naturalized into that people. The basis of this existence without prior essence is the withdrawal from a land in favor of a genealogy: for Jews, where you are born does not matter, only to whom.[8]

Benedict Anderson has movingly written of the human desire for continuity, expressed in "links between the dead and the yet unborn," adding that "the disadvantage of evolutionary/progressive thought is an almost Heraclitean hostility to any idea of continuity." He continues by pointing out that with the sunset of religious modes of thought, other modes of "transformation of fatality into continuity, contingency into meaning" became almost necessary. And Anderson concludes these reflections by declaring that "few things were (are) better suited to this end than an idea of nation."[9]

A Jew is not asked whether or not they wishes to be a Jew. There's no way to stop being Jewish, no escape from Jewishness. No one born Jewish is given a choice not to be Jewish; that is what marks off Jewishness theoretically from Christianness and is the reason why the statement "My parents were Jewish, but I'm not" is so much more startling than "My parents were Christians, but I'm not." There may be various means of getting into a family, including marriage and adoption, but it is very hard to get out of one.

Jean-Paul Sartre articulated brilliantly the meaning of this thrownness: " 'The Jew,' Sartre writes, 'cannot choose not to be a Jew. . . . To be a Jew is to be thrown into—to be *abandoned* to—the situation of a Jew; and at the same time it is to be responsible in and through one's person for the destiny and the very nature of the Jewish People.' "[10] And Sartre continues: "The authentic Jew, *makes himself a Jew*, in the face of all and against all" (emphasis in the original).[11] Lest there be any misunderstanding, neither Sartre nor certainly I attempt an assault on the absolute juridical liberty of any Jew to take up or deliver themself (*sic*) of this responsibility. The most common way of entering a family is to be born into one, thrown into the world always already with these connections that Rosenzweig is noting as characteristic of Jewishness, marking its difference from Christian thinking, in which the infant is an autonomous monad. Rosenzweig scholar Haggai Dagan has compellingly argued that for Rosenzweig, discourse is not rational in the Hegelian sense, but narrative/mythic "paint[ing] a picture," and thus, "according to such interpretation, terms like 'blood' and 'procreation' are part of a picturesque image, an image of self enfolded, a religious, enthusiastic existence."[12] This is what renders Jewry eternal and at the same time guarantees there is nothing in the essence of *Judaïté*. As a matter of lived experience, of course Jews can be as bad as other folks sometimes are and as good as the best of humanity without it changing their status as Jews. The Talmud already said this: "An Israelite, even were they to sin, remains an Israelite." Rosenzweig draws this out to a philosophical limit point, writing famously (or infamously), "The people of Israel does not have to hire the services of the spirit; the natural propagation of the body guarantees its eternity," correctly glossed by Dagan as "The Jewish people does not rely upon the spirit [in the Hegelian sense], nor upon intellectual or ethical uniqueness, nor upon one or another mental quality, but upon blood ties and natural procreation alone."[13]

Judaïté as Performance

For Rosenzweig, the *fact* of genealogy is what confers *Judaïté*. However, while *Judaïté* for him is an existence with no *necessary* essence, it is also the call of other Jews, the living and the dead, that constitutes the Jew. As Haggai Dagan has said: "Rosenzweig attributes great significance to culture and tradition, to ritual and to ways of thinking, even in the case of the uniqueness of the Jewish people. But this does not detract from the definitive nature" of the absolute absence of essence as the foundation of Jewish identity. How are we to take these two seemingly disparate accounts—of existence with no essential characteristics and the particular characteristics of a rich and varied cultural history?

One who is born a Jew also is born into the community of Jews, the Jewish nation. When Benedict Anderson famously defined nations as imagined communities, he imagined his imagined communities in space: a family, their neighbors, then the people of the next valley, and then all the valleys all the way to Paris are part of such a community. The Jewish nation, however, is a community imagined in time, not space. It is formed from my connection with my grandmother, to her mother, and hers until I have included all the generations in my imagined community in time all the way back to Mother Sarah (and her consort Abraham of course). Unlike a community that is formed in space, which can retain its identity while changing over time, expanding or contracting, what is formed in time exists and retains its identity only by repetition. As Duke University anthropologist/historian Engseng Ho puts it, "What matters is that the dispersed understand themselves to be linked by bonds, usually those of kinship." However, "Such bonds exist and endure, rather than atrophying, only so long as people continue to speak, sing, recite, read, write, narrate, and otherwise represent them."[14] The fact of genealogy may be what confers *Judaïté*, and all the rest are representations of it, but the representation must be nurtured to perdure. Rosenzweig's radical and nonracist account of the thrownness of being a Jew is based on the same fundamental structure—the bonds are primary and the representations secondary, almost superstructural.[15] The content of that existence is filled by such representations, by the collective and historical memory of much, much more than a memory of martyrdom—a historical collective identity.

This is not to say that the relocation of the Jews from a place-based to a generation-based, genealogical belonging does not pose problems at the same time that it is powerfully liberating from other kinds of problems. Oppression can shift from that visited upon external "others" to oppression of internal others—for example, women.[16] The most obvious site where that occurs is the mark of circumcision. However, circumcision is a cultural inscription, a representation, not itself a fact of being of gender or even of being gendered, but a representation of that difference. On the one hand, that "covenant placed into our flesh," insofar as "flesh" is penises, surely seems to exclude women. The very fact that Jewishness can *only* be conferred by a Jewish mother—only the son of a Jewish mother is to be circumcised, not the son of a Jewish father—carries some powerful counterforce, but this hardly seems a sufficient response on its own: "This community rooted in blood, is first and foremost the responsibility of the woman, who gives birth, who gives life" is not, of course, any kind of a feminist message or even amelioration.[17] On the other hand, matrilineal genealogy, like circumcision, also is not a fact of gender, but a representation. Both mark participation in a community, but a community of a particular kind, a community that simply, ontologically, is. Rosenzweig called the foundation of that community "blood," the opposite of blood and soil, blood that is possible only by renouncing the soil. So what, we may ask, is the relationship between that existence and the gendered representations of it? At this point, one needs to ask again, this time with Dagan, "why Rosenzweig saw fit to emphasize the matter of blood so strongly."[18]

Dagan writes compellingly: "In the context in which these things are stated, blood serves as a metaphor for stability, non-dependence, being gathered in upon oneself. The people are gathered within their own existence. The meaning of redemption for Rosenzweig is that the Jew is cut off from the world that surrounds him. He lives practically within history, but essentially outside of it."[19] This becomes clearer when we remember Anidjar's point given just above. The metaphor of blood is not, we contend, a metaphor of essence, but of circulation. Being of the "same blood" refers to circulating together in a closed symbolic system (not closed, of course, to others who might join).

In fact, though, there are two descriptions at work here at the same time: one of the pure fact of the closed system of genealogy symbolized by the circulation of blood and another composed of the shared discourse and practices that constitute historic Jewish cultural life. The two kinds of descriptions need to be read together, if not reconciled, but the danger—not the necessity, but the danger—of falling into racism is always present, especially when one speaks of blood.

To avoid that danger, we need a better way to understand their relationship. To get there, it is necessary to take our analysis beyond Rosenzweig. In the light of some of the most exciting theorization of sex/gender of the last three decades, that of Judith Butler and her followers, we may begin to move into a new direction of theorizing about kinship, generation, and diaspora.

In speaking of representations of difference—of Jewish difference— as constitutive of that difference, rather than the putative biological facts of gender and race, I am arguing that, as anthropologist Paul Rabinow put it so pellucidly a quarter century ago, "representations are social facts" with as much weight as any other fact and as much a claim on the nature of identities.[20] I want to move beyond even the radically correct insights of Rosenzweig and treat representations as the primary force generating diasporic identities, including the representation that constitutes the imagined community in time, namely, kinship.[21] I want to disturb any hierarchy that imagines the genealogical bonds as somehow more "real" than the representations, arguing that it is the representations that produce the bonds and bring them into being as a kind of reality. Paralleling the classic move that feminist philosopher Judith Butler made vis-à-vis sex and gender, I suggest that the bonds themselves are always already (as we used to speak) a representation; the ties of kinship that produce the imagined community of the diasporic nation are part and parcel of the representations, produced by the representations, and not productive of them.

Seen in this way, what I call *Judaïté* is the performance of being Jewish, because existence within the community produced by its representations is performative. As Judith Butler has defined it, performativity "seeks to counter a certain kind of positivism according to which we might begin with already delimited understandings" of what we seek to understand, including gender and other kinds of identity. It "starts to describe a set of processes that produce ontological effects, that is, that work to bring into being certain kinds of realities or . . . that lead to certain kinds of socially binding consequences."[22]

Treating identity as performance challenges the physical, real, or factual existence of a given cultural category, such as gender, and argues for (not demonstrates) its constructedness by what human actors do. It asserts that it is the process of repeated performance of certain practices that constitutes the internal sense of belonging to a category, constructing that belonging socially as a shared and given identity with "socially binding consequences." Performativity thus delineates a theory and a process. Following the same analysis, I want to claim here that it is repeated and reiterated performance that produces the internal sense of being a Jew and of being connected particularly (not exclusively) with other Jews and that thus constitutes a Jewish diasporic nation.

We now can explain in a different manner how representations (practices) are tied to bonds (of kinship), understanding that because the representations produce the bonds, they do not merely sustain or vivify them. The ties that bind are not lies that bind (although they can be, of course), but rather powerful effects of representations and performances that give rise to the internal—and very powerful—sense of kinship and identity. Kinship and identity themselves function something like the internal movements that, deriving their power from performance, construct gendered senses of selves as well, according to Butler. As Butler has put it, "The point is not simply that such an 'effect' is compounded through repetition, but that reiteration is the means through which that effect is established anew, time and again."23

Precisely. The practices that constitute Jewish identity—and perhaps more broadly ethnic or national identities in general, *mutatis mutandis*—consist of the speaking of Jewish languages or the use of markedly Jewish forms of language (Throw Mama from the train—a kiss), modes of walking, body language, telling stories, singing songs, as well as the study of Talmud, practicing the rituals of the holidays, eating this food and not that. The sharing of these repetitious performances is what produces kinship bonds.24 Here I must again refer to Patricia Williams's perfect description cited above, that it is not biology that produces ancestral bonds but "the inheritance of linguistically and rhetorically embedded traditions passed on in habits of speech. I am composed of the voices of those who bred me. We are talked into the world by our forebears: by how they parsed words or not."

None of these performances apply to all Jews, nor need they. At the very beating heart of such narratives, practices, representations, scripts, doings, all the performances that produce *Judaïté*, are Torah, primarily, but not necessarily or only the study of the Talmud (with all of its ramifications for forms of Jewish speech and speech practices), and the *performance* of the Jewish doings, whether or not they are conceived of as divine commandments. As that Torah itself reminds us: "Forever let a person study the Torah even not for its own sake, for from such study, they will come to study for its own sake."25

In the next chapter, I will deepen and, I hope, further clarify my search for a universalist noncosmopolitanism via some, I reckon, illuminating comparisons.

4
Judaïtude/Négritude

I'm not going to confine myself to some narrow particularism.
But I do not intend either to become lost in a disembodied
universalism. . . . I have a different idea of a universal. It is a universal rich with all that is particular, rich with all the particulars there
are, the deepening of each particular, the coexistence of them all.

Aimé Césaire, Député for Martinique, to Maurice Thorez,
Secretary General of the French Communist Party, October 1956

In this quotation that I cite again here as a kind of watchword or
talisman, the great Afro-Caribbean poet, thinker, and statesman Aimé
Césaire eschews a certain version of cosmopolitanism, the kind that
seeks to deracinate deep and important differences in *Lebensformen*
between different human groups and somehow always advances a
universal morality that is consistent with the mores of the dominant
political and ethnic group. At the same time, he refuses ideas of the
superiority or supremacy of one collective over others, any others.
Césaire was one of the great exponents and developers of the theoretical and practical movement that he named Négritude, insisting on
the great value of African and black cultures, as against discourses that
claimed that black folk need to aspire to becoming full participants in
Western European white culture.[1] An *Encyclopedia Britannica* definition captures the motive of this influential movement concisely:

These views inspired many of the basic ideas behind Négritude: that the mystic warmth of African life, gaining strength from its closeness to nature and its constant contact with ancestors, should be continually placed in proper perspective against the soullessness and materialism of Western culture; that Africans must look to their own cultural heritage to determine the values and traditions that are most useful in the modern world; that committed writers should use African subject matter and poetic traditions and should excite a desire for political freedom; that Négritude itself encompasses the whole of African cultural, economic, social, and political values; and that, above all, the value and dignity of African traditions and peoples must be asserted.

In this chapter, I will propose that Négritude and the controversies around it provide a consequential point of comparison with Jewish discourses of identity and cultural preservation in modernity as I, like Césaire, stand for opposition to assimilation without assertion of supremacy. I have coined yet another term to signify these elective affinities: *Judaïtude*. To clear up any confusion that I introduce by doing so, let me distinguish between this new term and *Judaïté*. While *Judaïté* is the term I am using in this manifesto for English "Jewishness" and "Judaism," *Judaïtude* is being employed by me as the name of a particular approach or even politics of *Judaïté*, in some ways analogous to Césaire's *Négritude*.

Lest I be misunderstood, I will state here and elsewhere that I am not proposing equivalence—moral, political, or otherwise—between the so-called black experience and the equally so-called Jewish experience, such equivalences being always apologetic and whitewashing, as it were. I do submit that Jews have much to learn from Africana theorists and controversies, just as these latter have learned in the postwar period from Jewish history and its controversies.

Césaire's declaration appears in a letter responding to a controversy between Sartre, Lévi-Strauss, and Fanon in which Sartre had offered a dialectical image in which the "Negro" and "Négritude" would be sublated (the synthesis that overcomes a negated element in a dialectic) into the unmarked-for-race working-class struggle.[2] As critic Haun Saussy determines, "For Frantz Fanon, this scenario of the future *Aufhebung* (dialectical sublation) of race implied the *Aufhebung* (cancellation) of his history and identity—a grimly negative reading that saw the cannibal qualities of Sartre's Hegelian optimism."[3] Fanon is responding to this declaration in Sartre's *Black Orpheus*: "In fact, Négritude appears as the weak stage of a dialectical progression: the theoretical and practical affirmation of white supremacy is the thesis; the position of Négritude as antithetical value is the moment of negativity. But this negative moment is not sufficient in itself and the Blacks who employ it well know it; they know that it serves to pave the way for the synthesis or the realization of the human society without race. Thus Négritude is dedicated to its own destruction, it is transition and not result, a means and not the ultimate goal."[4]

In this writing, Sartre explicitly interprets an assertion of black identity, Négritude, as solely a stage in a development, a stage to be transcended and ultimately cancelled, in philosophical terms "sublated," that is, assimilated and then left behind. Fanon writes, "When I read this page, I felt they had robbed me of my last chance."[5] Last chance for what? For Négritude! Négritude itself—blackness, with whatever values it comprised for Fanon.[6]

I judge this reading as compelling, if certainly not the only possible one.[7] It is certainly the one that moves me, because that last chance for powerful and just Jewish identity is being robbed by those such as Appiah—now, as I write. As Fanon said, "What is certain is that, at the very moment when I was trying to grasp my own being, Sartre, who remained The Other, gave me a name and thus shattered my last illusion." "The last illusion, last chance" is for a Césairian universalism that does not demand sameness, an *Aufhebung* that does not realize human society without race.[8]

A closer reading of Fanon's *Black Skin, White Masks* helps expound this point. In his foreword to the English translation, Kwame Anthony Appiah has referred appositely to Fanon's "dialogue with Négritude, then the dominant system of thought among black francophone intellectuals." On the one hand, Fanon seriously critiqued the ascription of a particular sort of mind to black folks, arguing that this is precisely a European (and racist) fantasy. However, at the same time, Fanon "conceded that Négritude could play an important role in freeing the native intellectual of dependence on metropolitan culture," and clearly, I would add, not as a negative moment in a dialectic, an antithesis.[9] Otherwise how to explain his sickened response to Sartre? At any rate, it is crucial not to miss Fanon's "The black man who strives to whiten his race is as wretched as the one who preaches hatred of the white man," interpreted recently by Robert Bernasconi: "To renounce his race is not an option for Fanon."[10] Fanon, like Césaire, both Marxists, seeks justice for all the wretched of the earth, but not at the expense of his Négritude. Having learned much from Fanon as well as from Césaire, I want to go into more detail here on Négritude, especially Fanon's response to it, and also to think about *Judaïtude* and race.

Fanon's struggles with Négritude are well known. It is indeed with regard to Négritude that he marks the following ambivalence:

> The educated black man, slave of the myth of the spontaneous and cosmic Negro, feels at some point in time that his race no longer understands him.
>
> Or that he no longer understands his race.

He is only too pleased about this, and by developing further this difference, this incomprehension and discord, he discovers the meaning of his true humanity. Less commonly he wants to feel a part of his people. And with feverish lips and frenzied heart he plunges into the great black hole. We shall see that this wonderfully generous attitude rejects the present and future in the name of a mystical past.[11]

This is a very prickly and difficult passage indeed. I want to propose as a working hypothesis that Fanon's dilemma is not entirely unrelated to that of the Sage Hillel, who said: "If I am not for myself, who will be for me, and if I am for myself, what good am I?" and who then followed it up with a call to action, namely, "And if not now, when?!" (Mishna Avot 1:14). (Fanon's expression of the problem is "the black man's dimension of being-for-others.")[12] If one wishes to erase one's "race," it is, as we've seen above, as disgusting to Fanon as preaching hatred of the white man, and here the desire for and pleasure in incomprehension of his race, in which "he discovers the meaning of his true humanity" (which I take as irony), is nearly as troubling as "the great black hole." Fanon's expressed disgust at the alleged development of drugs to whiten the skin also speaks to this reading as making sense of Fanon's nausea.

Fanon's *Judaïté*

In the stunning fifth chapter of *Black Skin, White Masks*, Fanon explicitly works out a genealogy of his self and his progress to and through Négritude. Less surprising to me now than it would have been once, this Bildungsroman is deeply involved with *Judaïté* as well. He initiates this part of his account by declaring, "It's in the name of tradition that the anti-Semites base their 'point of view.' "[13] Fanon goes on to remark that it might seem strange to equate anti-Semitism with negrophobia, but then recounts how and when he had been taught that equation, namely, by his philosophy teacher in the Antilles, who asserted clearly: "When you hear someone insulting the Jews, pay attention; he is talking about you." And Fanon assents, "Since then, I have understood that what he meant quite simply was that the anti-Semite is inevitably a negrophobe." Strikingly, and without further elaboration at this point, it is precisely here in his tale of self that Fanon "finally made up my mind to shout my blackness." In the next two pages or so, with enrapturing quotations from Senghor and Césaire, Fanon evokes (ruefully? somewhat ironically?) the excitement of that youthful shout of blackness from his throat as well as the depths of its dangers, "the great black hole" of which he has warned. But, this moment concludes: "Yes, we . . . are backward, naive, and free. For us the body is not in opposition to what you call the soul. We are in the world. And long live the bond between Man and the Earth! Moreover, our writers have helped me to convince you that your white civilization lacks a wealth of subtleness and sensitivity."[14] And he continues, citing Senghor on "Negro emotion."

Fanon evokes brilliantly, thrillingly, the excitement of the young black man—himself—who discovered Senghor and his version of Négritude. But then: "I was soon to become disillusioned."[15] All of that beautiful emotion and rhythm, all that Négritude, was ascribed by whites to the earlier stages of the human race that they had already superseded (and I use that term on my own advice). The next stage of Fanon's ascribed self-genealogy involves the African pride of another form of Négritude, the glorying in the great black civilizations of the past.[16] But that also was contemned by the whites: "I couldn't hope to win. I tested my heredity. I did a complete checkup of my sickness. I wanted to be typically black—that was out of the question. I wanted to be white—that was a joke. And when I tried to claim my Négritude intellectually as a concept, they snatched it away from me."[17]

And with this, we arrive at Sartre. It is indeed Sartre who has robbed Fanon of his negritude (his very blackness), even more than of his Négritude: "We had appealed to a friend of the colored peoples, and this friend had found nothing better to do than demonstrate the relativity of their action." By "relativity," of course, Fanon means precisely that negative, merely antithetical, cancelable (sublatable) moment in the dialectic: "While I, in a paroxysm of experience and rage, was proclaiming this [Senghorian Négritude], he [Sartre] reminded me that my Négritude was nothing but a weak stage.[18] Truthfully, I'm telling you, I sensed my shoulder slipping from this world, and my feet no longer felt the caress of the ground. Without a black past, without a black future, it was impossible for me to live my blackness."[19] And yet, "with all my being, I refuse to accept this amputation."[20] Fanon scholar Reiland Rabaka has glossed this passage powerfully: "Fanon found Sartre's Hegelization of Négritude not only paternalist, but also indicative of his infantilization of blacks, the 'childhood of the world.' "[21]

But I must give Sartre his due here (or at least a partial payment on what is due him), for he does not simply—or even not at all—fit into the camp of those cosmopolitans who do wish the Jews as an entity, as an epistemic object, would simply disappear from the world, nor the camp of those who claim that it is the very insistence of the Pariah People on their own survival that is the cause of anti-Semitism.[22] El'ad Lapidot shows how Sartre's shocking declaration that it is the anti-Semite who makes the Jew is deeply related to his position on collective identity. Sartre begins from a negation of Jews as having a historical consciousness, but "nevertheless identifies, beyond physiology . . . a factually existent French Jewish consciousness, namely a collective Jewish episteme," or form of knowledge.[23] However: "Since the historical Jewish episteme has been lost without a trace, current Jewish consciousness for Sartre necessarily derives from a non-Jewish consciousness, 'the Jew is one whom other men consider a Jew.' "[24] Once, however, one understands that this is the condition of all consciousness for Sartre, that the very nature of human consciousness is that it "acquires a positive and factual being through its 'being for others,' i.e., the process of being perceived and treated in certain ways by other people, through 'the look of the other,' " then, at any rate, the seeming hostility to Jewish consciousness is much ameliorated.[25] We begin to grasp how "for Sartre the creation of the Jew through the anti-Semite transpires as a paradigm for the normal way in which collective identities are created. Consequently, . . . the understanding that the Jew is created by the anti-Semite does not lead Sartre to renounce this creation but on the contrary to acknowledge it, to give it recognition." And hence, Sartre is deeply opposed to what he calls "the Democrats"— I think we would call them neoliberals—who decline all collectivities and recognize only individuals (the Cologne court, some American theoreticians), "solving the 'Jewish Question' by simply saying: 'There are no Jews.' "[26]

Looking for a way through the aporia, the dead end, Fanon has traversed this inner journey of anguish, beginning with Jews and indeed with his solidarity with Jews, the Jews being the ultimate sublatables of Christendom. Jews are good for thinking with for Fanon, and Fanon is good for thinking with for me, the Jew.[27]

The Deracinated of the Earth

A human being has roots by virtue of his real, active, and natural participation in the life of a community, which preserves in living shape certain particular treasures of the past and certain particular expectations for the future. . . . The loss of the past, whether it be collectively or individually, is the supreme human tragedy.

Simone Weil

The attempt to think about the aporias of *Judaïté* alongside of blackness here, the endeavor to be taught by black thinkers, is, thus, generated in part via Fanon's own observations on the nexus between *Judaïté* and blackness.[28]

> Colonial racism is no different from other racisms.
> Anti-Semitism cuts me to the quick; I get upset; a frightful rage makes me anemic; they are denying me the right to be a man. I cannot dissociate myself from the fate reserved for my brother. Every one of my acts commits me as a man. Every instance of my reticence, every instance of my cowardice, manifests the man.[29]

Lest it need pointing out—and it seems it does—once again, my point is not to make an equivalence, either historical nor moral, between the Sho'ah and the Middle Passage or anti-Semitism and racism, nor certainly to justify anyone's bad behavior (Zionism), but to see what can be learned from putting Jewishness and blackness in conversation with each other. (An early anonymous reader suggested that the point of this writing was to propose that since blacks can have nationalism, Jews can too. I intend this direct denial to dispel such a reading.)

Fanon teaches us the dilemma posed by desire for decolonized identity, as African, as Jew, and the disasters that ensue when one falls into the black hole of an exclusive identity politics. On a personal level—and the only evidence I offer here is my own experience—the descriptions that Fanon gives of the black man desiring whiteness have been matched in my life with a desire for goyness in very similar ways to those that Fanon describes.

The most remarkable passage in *Black Skin, White Masks* regarding the ligature between Jews and blacks is the following. I quote it here *in toto* so that its power and complexity can be encountered, and then I'll discuss it at some length, at the length it deserves, to the best of my ability:

> The Jewishness [*Judaïté*] of the Jew, however, can go unno-
> ticed. He is not integrally what he is. We can but hope and
> wait. His acts and behavior are the determining factor. He is
> a white man, and apart from some debatable features, he can
> pass undetected. He belongs to the race that has never prac-
> ticed cannibalism. What a strange idea, to eat one's father!
> Serves them right; they shouldn't be black. Of course the Jews
> have been tormented—what am I saying? They have been
> hunted, exterminated, and cremated, but these are just minor
> episodes in the family history. The Jew is not liked as soon as
> he has been detected. But with me things take on a *new* face.
> I'm not given a second chance. I am overdetermined from the
> outside. I am a slave not to the "idea" that others have of me,
> but to my appearance.[30]

Fanon's ambivalence with regard to the Jew here is tangible, and it oscillates around the idea of "passing." On the one hand, he produces here, as in several places throughout the book, expressions of the most categorical solidarity and comparability with Jews, but in this famous passage, that solidarity is tinged with something else, something that Fanon detects in himself and is shocked at: "Of course the Jews have been tormented—what am I saying? They have been hunted, exter-minated, and cremated, but these are just minor episodes in the fam-ily history." That's because Jews are firmly identified here with "whites" owing to their alleged possibility of passing, "apart from some debatable features." (Does Fanon here mean "Jewish noses"? Fanon apparently knew nothing of Jews of color, but that is another problem.) The text itself is dismayed by this sudden disavowal. I want to propose that here, as in many places, Fanon is marking through the Jew his own ambivalence between asserting his black identity and wishing to escape it, envious for the moment, it seems, of the Jew, who allegedly can escape their identity, apart from those debatable features. As support for this reading, let me quote again: "The black man who strives to whiten his race is . . . wretched."

Fanon also uses this difference between the allegedly white Jew and the black man to generate, construct, and justify treating the black man as a single category, as opposed to the "Hova, the Moor, Tuareg, Fula, or Bantu": "The universal situation of the black man is ambiguous, but this is resolved in his physical existence. This in a way puts him beside the Jew. In order to counter the alleged obstacles above, we shall resort to the obvious fact that *wherever he goes, a black man remains a black man.*"[31] The Jew has no such features that mark them always and everywhere and therefore—what, precisely? They can choose to disappear, to put on French, British, or German masks.

As I have learned myself, this "whiteness" or invisibility of the Jew is a trap as well as a refuge. Perhaps I sat on a train at a time in my life when I was not so detectable as a Jew and sitting across from me in the subway car was a Hassid from Brooklyn. A child cries out, "Look, Mom, look, a Jew! Dirty. Ikh." If I am silent at that moment, I have alienated myself from myself; if I speak, then I have been "detected." The epistemology of the closet. Despite Fanon's envy of the Jew's alleged possibility of disappearance—notoriously, it didn't work too well among the Nazis—he, too, understands well the psychic cost of deracination.

Toward the Diaspora Nation

"If we are for ourselves, what good are we?" We Jews have seen the calamities wrought by not pursuing any solidarity beyond the racial or national (especially in the Israeli state and sickeningly now (summer 2021), producing the dilemma or even paradox "If I am not for myself, who will be for me, but if I am for myself, what good am I?" But to that, the Sage added: "And if not now, when?!" Something must be done.

As that something, I offer the dual loyalties and doubled culture of the Diaspora Nation. The Diaspora Nation as a model suggests another way, leading to (never perfectly, of course) ardent transterritorial collective solidarity—the nonsovereign nation—and ardent solidarity, as well, with proximate others—the local oppressed class/proletariat, racial group, BLM (none of these an abstraction at all)—at the same time.[32]

Let us imagine now disaggregating nation from state. It is, after all, only recently that the concepts of nation and state have begun to collapse into each other.[33] In his concept history, word history, of *nación* in Spanish usage, E .J. Hobsbawm has shown that it was only in 1884 that the association of "nation" with "a State or political body" appeared in the dictionary of the Spanish Academy.[34] Even then, it didn't settle there, since in the final edition of that textual monument from 1925, a nation is defined as "the collectivity of persons who have the same ethnic origin and, in general, speak the same language and possess a common tradition."[35] In other words, in that linguistic/cultural world, the association of nations with states, as an integral part of their being nations, was late and contested.[36] Hobsbawm makes the same point with respect to other languages, including German and Dutch, summing up:

> The problem of the relation of even such an extended but indigenous "nation" to the state remained puzzling, *for it seemed evident that in ethnic, linguistic or any other terms, most states of any size were not homogeneous, and could therefore not simply be equated with nations* [emphasis added]. The Dutch

dictionary specifically singles out as a peculiarity of the French and English that they use the word "nation" to mean the people belonging to a state even when not speaking the same language. . . . From this it follows that it can have no territorial meaning, since members of different nations (divided by "differences in ways of life—*Lebensarten*—and customs") can live together in the same province, even quite a small one.[37]

The upshot of this is that "nation" has a much longer history, even within modernity itself, in the nonterritorial, nonstate sense, than we assume. I couldn't imagine a more trenchant statement of the state of the "nation" than Hobsbawm's: "Whatever the 'proper and original' or any other meaning of 'nation,' the term is clearly still quite different from its modern meaning. We may, thus, without entering further into the matter, accept that in its modern and basically political sense the concept *nation* is historically very young."[38] If the evident toxicity of both nation and nationalism is a product of the inexorable association with sovereignty, the nation-state, then imagining a form of national existence that is explicitly countersovereign—unstated, we could say—might be a way to save the nation as an aggregation of folks with a common *Lebensart* and stories about themselves and each other.[39] This is my schema to save the Nation of the Jews.

My insistence on using the word "nation" puzzles—and even repels—many of my associates, colleagues, and friends and very likely many of you, my readers, as well. As leading Indian postcolonial theorist Partha Chatterjee has characterized the current discursive situation of "nationalism," it was

by the 1970s, the reason why people in the Third World killed each other—sometimes in wars between regular armies, sometimes, more distressingly, in cruel and often protracted civil wars, and increasingly, it seemed, by technologically sophisticated and virtually unstoppable acts of terrorism. The leaders of the African struggles against colonialism and racism had spoiled their records by becoming heads of corrupt, fractious, and often brutal regimes; Gandhi had been appropriated by such marginal cults as pacifism and vegetarianism; and even Ho Chi Minh, in his moment of glory, was caught in the unyielding polarities of the Cold War. Nothing, it would seem, was left in the legacy of nationalism to make people in the Western world feel good about it.[40]

No wonder my friends and relations are, almost to a person, appalled by my vaunting of a nationalism, any nationalism. In this manifesto, I hope to save the nation by demonstrating the continued vitality (creative energies) and utility (force for good) of this term in thinking about human collective lives.

We miss nearly everything that is important and alive in the nation when we focus only on sovereignty. Nationalism is so much more than that; indeed, I hold that it is everything without it. Chatterjee points to the ways that the early nationalism conceived of "the 'spiritual' or 'inner' aspects of culture, such as language or religion or the elements of personal and family life" as the proper realm of the nation, while the "outer" domain of the state, the "material domain of law, administration, economy, and statecraft," had to be the same for the colonized nation as for the colonizers. The distinction is indeed crucial, but it simply cannot be mapped onto an "inner"—or worse, "spiritual"—dimension versus an "outer" or "material" one. Education, for instance, is just as material as an army or central bank. Insofar as we desire merely to give a historical account, it may be correct to refer to such distinctions, for it seems that thinkers did—then—and indeed, we will see that distinction reproduced in Jewish discourse as the differentiation between the "political" and the "cultural" in Zionism.[41] Insofar, however, as I am committed to a deliberative rhetoric here, a discourse of "what is to be done," there is no doubt in my mind that the terms need to be thoroughly revised, eschewing any oppositions between the material/political and the spiritual or cultural.

In place of what Chatterjee sees as the "spiritual" or the "inner" aspects of collective existence, I prefer to think of "autonomy," which is as political a term as the "sovereignty" of the state apparatuses with which he contrasts it. I mean here autonomy in the sense of group autonomy, the retention by a collective of its (or major aspects of its) form of life, its culture, not static, as in a museum, but vital, developing, changing, and growing such that the collective is always recognizable as a version of itself. I am thinking of an autonomy that allows for a collective to retain its collective existence, identity, representations, and practices (not, to be sure, with no limits) within a context of sovereignty shared with others, something like—I dare to think— what Mahatma Gandhi desired for India. "Consent not to be a single being," as Édouard Glissant put it.[42] Again, I emphasize that this autonomy is not only inner, hidden, or psychospiritual, but as much a form of political practice as sovereignty itself and compatible—or better put, a free variable—with it.[43]

The material life of the nation, the so-called political, is always present. The pivotal question is how the members of different "nations" can coexist in the same spaces in ways that are productive for all. How do we get to Césaire's "the coexistence of them all"? It will be seen immediately—I hope—that putting the question in these terms and having rejected neoliberal cosmopolitanism and racial "ethnic cleansing" (hard or soft) from the realm of possibilities makes the distinction between political and cultural dimensions inoperable and indeed anachronistic. Then it becomes clear that it is the focus on monoethnic sovereignty that is the problem, not the focus on the nation per se.

The most important historical insight of recent historiography is that Jewish nationalism was not, by any means, identified with the state until quite late in its history and very near to the founding of that state. Surprisingly—at least I was surprised—the separation of nation and state occurred in the Jewish movement *now* most identified with the nation-state, Zionism. Zionism is taken today as precisely the movement that successfully led to the Jewish State of Israel, that is, the very apotheosis of Jewish statist-nationalism. Seemingly at first paradoxically, as the next chapter will show, a survey of some vitally important recent scholarship on the early history of Zionism—and especially two of its most canonical figures—helps make the case for the nation sans sovereignty, for what I call the no-state solution.[44]

5

Zionism without Israel

I am, needless to say by now, not only an anti-Zionist, opposed to the Jewish state or the state of the Jews, but opposed to all nation-states, that is, to states that are founded on the principle that they belong to one nation and that one nation belongs to a certain territory. That is why arguments that take the form "Well, everyone else has one, so if you're against the Jews having a nation-state, you're an anti-Semite" carry no water as far as I am concerned: I am against all nation-states. The tight association between the nation and the state is a relatively new and modern concept that makes it—perhaps—more dislodgeable than we imagine. In this chapter, following some of the cutting-edge recent historiography of Zionism, I'll discuss the startling but ultimately compelling proposition that the most canonical early thinkers of Zionism were not proponents of the nation-state, but generated the idea of the stateless nation as solution to the "Jewish Question"—diaspora as the *answer* to the Jewish Question, not itself the question.[1] I am speaking here of at least two of the most canonical and iconic names in the history of the Zionist movement, Theodor Herzl (1860–1904) and Asher Ginzberg (Ahad Ha'am, 1856–1920).

If that's true, you may well ask, what is it that makes them Zionists at all? It is their commitment to an autonomous Jewish region within Palestine, not a state, and certainly not a state that covers or claims all of Palestine. I am not supporting even that vision, but I think seeing this point helps create a wedge between the nationalism

I do espouse and the notion that nationalism must or certainly ought to implicate statist control of a particular territory. I do not here intend a defense of Zionism in any form; what I am trying to show is that even classical Zionism did not envision a state dominated by one ethnos, the Jews, nor certainly the ethnic cleansing that is being enacted right now, as I write.

Partha Chatterjee remarks, "If the nation is an imagined community and if nations must also take the form of states, then our theoretical language must allow us to talk about community and state at the same time."[2] On the contrary, there is no reason to assume a priori that "nations must also take the form of states." Or rather, that is *the* question, the new Jewish Question.

What if nations do not have to take the form of states? What if the Jewish nation, I inquire, could remain productively creative, vibrant, exciting, alive, while being equivalently alive to the needs and desires of others than Jews? This actually seems to have been the dream of the earliest forms of the Jewish nationalist movement known as Zionism. As Jerusalem historian Dmitry Shumsky has demonstrated compellingly in his eye-opening recent book, *Beyond the Nation-State*, neither Asher Ginzberg (Ahad Ha'am) nor even Theodor Herzl had even dreamed of a Jewish state in the modern sense, opting instead, each in his separate fashion, for a Jewish autonomous region, with perhaps the vast majority of Jews in the world remaining outside that area, a sort of *Gaeltacht*, if you will.[3]

The Culture of Theodor Herzl

In the historiopoesis of Zionism, these two major thinkers have been assigned Chatterjee's roles of "nationalism as a political movement" and "spiritual nationalism" or "cultural nationalism." At least in one feature, this categorization is correct. Herzl's was a "cultural nationalism"—his Zionism was in this sense cultural, just not anything recognizable to me as "Jewish" culture.

Herzl did not care at all for Jewish difference; in fact, he rejected it entirely, infamously writing in his diaries, "I am a German-speaking Jew from Hungary and can never be anything but a German. At present I am not recognized as a German. But that will come once we are over there." It is not insignificant that Herzl, himself originally a Hungarian Austrian, identifies himself explicitly as a German and not as an Austro-Hungarian or whatever the alternative to German might have been. He is a German because that is the language he speaks and the culture to which he is committed. This has little to do with Bismarck or Prussia, however. He expects to be a German in Palestine! This is borne out in Herzl's famous "utopian" novel, *Altneuland* (Oldnewland), depicting the fulfillment of a Zionist state in which that "Jewish" state is, in fact, a perfect copy of the German metropolis: at the opera they performed operas on biblical themes, and the Alexanderer Wunder-Rebbe (a highly powerful Polish Hassidic leader) has been translated into the bishop of Haifa.[4]

Herzl's "Jewish state" is an autonomous part of a larger imperial or multinational democracy but, even so, surely not a state for all the Jews. Shumsky writes, "Herzl intended his 'Jewish state' to make it easier for the Jews who remained in their home countries to either assimilate completely or else maintain an exclusively religious form of Jewish identity."[5] The shocker here is that this research demonstrates Herzl to have been essentially a Jew in opposition to the Jewish nation-state. The Jewish state envisioned by Herzl was a substate autonomous region, which, as Shumsky shows, was what the term *Staat* meant at the time: "Most of the neighboring non-Jewish national movements of the Habsburg imperial space in Herzl's time used the term *Staat* with explicitly substatist intentions in their national political programs and position."[6]

Shumsky's revised and revisionist reading of the writings of those Jewish thinkers called Zionists— especially of Herzl, the putative godfather of the State of Israel—will meet with resistance, no doubt, but to this writer, the documentation and interpretations offered by Shumsky provide more than full evidence for the innovation in the mid-*twentieth* century of the concept of a Jewish fully sovereign nation-state in which all others who happen to be there are second-class citizens—at best. Let me clarify that by "innovation," I don't mean that no one had ever thought of it before, but that it is only then that it becomes practically synonymous with Jewish nationalism and especially with Zionism. In this respect, Herzl is no better or worse than the other Zionist writers. What is unique, perhaps, is his total disregard for the maintenance and continuing vitality and future of Jewish culture in all of its manifestations. In Herzl's Jews' state—"a non-Jewish state of Jews," in Shumsky's brilliant formulation—culture is fully German in its nature, thus giving space to the Jews back in Germany simply to *be* Germans of the Mosaic persuasion—if that.

Without going into detail on the reading of Herzl that supports these judgments (Shumsky's book is highly accessible for those interested), suffice it to say once more that the primary difference—if not the only major difference—between Herzl's dream of a state of the Jews and that of other nearly contemporary thinkers is that Herzl seemed to care very, very little indeed about the *Jewish* part of the state, seeking only to escape from harassment on the part of anti-Semites. Although not a politics of sovereignty, which would be read back into his writings only after the establishment of the state, it is the case, it seems, that for Herzl, as for the latter-day nationalists in the postcolonial world, all that matters are governmental structures of one sort or another, and not the cultural life of the nation, except insofar as it is mock German.[7]

As Shumsky emphasizes, however, this does not negate a cultural dimension to Herzlian Zionism; this is not a culturally neutral stance. Mock German is precisely the cultural formation that Herzl dreams of for the Jews.[8] He envisions not only such things as operas in German on biblical topics performed at the Jerusalem Opera and a Jewish bishop of Haifa, but duels fought by young men with swords—in short, a little postcolonial entity mimicking Central European *Bildung* and mores.[9] Although Shumsky provides an elaborate cultural context for Herzl, arguing that German culture was indeed a species of Jewish culture for him and his social group, nonetheless, Herzl's connection with any aspect of traditional (not a synonym for "religious") culture at all was tenuous, at best. I have written on this point at greater length elsewhere.[10] But see meanwhile Shumsky's report vis-à-vis Herzl that "the cultural homeland of the Zionist commonwealth is Europe and . . . there are no signs of any disconnect from this homeland that in any way resembles a move from and 'exile' to a 'Zion.' "[11]

Once again, I find Fanon's analyses very helpful in thinking this through: "All colonized people—in other words, people in whom an inferiority complex has taken root, whose local cultural originality has been committed to the grave—position themselves in relation to the civilizing language: i.e., the metropolitan culture. The more the colonized has assimilated the cultural values of the metropolis, the more he will have escaped the bush. The more he rejects his blackness and the bush, the whiter he will become."[12] Similarly for Herzl: the local cultural originality is in Hebrew and Yiddish (in Europe); the metropolitan language is German, as are the cultural values.[13] The bush is the ghetto, and the more he rejects his Jewishness and the ghetto, the "whiter" he will become.[14] "Whiten the race, save the race, but not along the lines you might think; do not safeguard 'the originality of that part of the world in which they grew up,' but ensure its whiteness." Ensure the Germanness of the Jews. The quotation from Herzl bears repeating: "I am a German-speaking Jew from Hungary and can never be anything but a German. At present I am not recognized as a German. But that will come once we are over there."[15]

The Politics of Ahad Ha'am

The other vitally important and paradigmatic Zionist thinker, Ahad Ha'am, in contrast, focuses acutely on Jewish cultural difference, vital and significant, and how it might be continued into the future within a political framework nearly identical to that envisioned by Herzl, substate autonomy in Palestine and elsewhere. What characterizes Ahad Ha'am's thought and makes it especially important now is the notion of full cultural life for the nation in contact with others and in spaces of shared sovereignty with other nations equally devoted to the fullness of their cultural, national futures. The purpose of this autonomy is entirely other to Herzl's. While for Herzl the stated purpose of getting away from the anti-Semites in Europe was to become culturally proper Germans, for Ahad Ha'am, it was to have space within which to produce a Hebrew, Jewish cultural modernity, deeply rooted in the ancient forms, languages, and practices of the past. He is, therefore, in Zionist historiography dubbed the founder of so-called cultural Zionism. This was not, I hasten to add, isolationist or chauvinist (not at all a "new Greece," in Herzl's infelicitous and contemptuous formulation). This autonomous region in Palestine was meant to be the epicenter of a constant renewal of a Jewish culture throughout the world wherever Jews lived as well.

Indeed, as Shumsky demonstrates compellingly, Ahad Ha'am's political thought has been consistently distorted by readings generated within the ideological paradigm of the Israeli nation-state that identifies the state as the only possible political telos for a Jewish nationalism that might claim the name Zionism. As he shows in his rich chapter on the political thought of Ahad Ha'am, this thinker's thought was as political as Herzl's—just as he had previously shown that Herzl's thought was as "cultural" as Ahad Ha'am's. On the political level, both imagined shared substate cultural autonomies in the territory of Palestine. It is on the cultural level that they diverged.

Herzl's commitment to a shared Central European–German culture for both Jews and Muslims in Palestine, it would seem, put less pressure on the idea of binational existence, while Ahad Ha'am's dream of a vibrant national culture for the Jews—worldwide, but with Palestine as its epicenter—required in fact considerably more thought on the political level, including Ahad Ha'am's explicit demand that rights must be equal for the two nations sharing the territory and the sovereignty. Shumsky establishes how consistent was Ahad Ha'am's vision of the contemporary situation of many peoples in their time and place: "In this reality, different nations sought to preserve and reinforce their particular identities while simultaneously maintaining economic relationships and day-to-day cultural loyalties within spaces that were shaped by a slew of different group identities."[16] In other words, Ahad Ha'am's vision of a Jewish cultural center that empowers and enlivens the cultural lives of Jews in many other places "had clear parallels in the lives of neighboring peoples in the imperial world. Indeed, it appears that the spiritual center idea was not at all disconnected from the concrete reality of Ahad Ha'am's time."[17] Ahad Ha'am himself gave the brilliant comparison with Warsaw, which was certainly the cultural epicenter of Polishness in music, in art, in thinking, and in language and literature while hardly being the economic or sovereign center of Polish life in the lands in which Poles lived, for example, Galicia, until 1918 a province of Austria. And this can be understood as the major contribution of Ahad Ha'am to an imagined Jewish future now. For Ahad Ha'am, erasing Jewish (Hebrew) culture was hardly a contribution to openness and pluralism; indeed, Herzl's slogan "regardless of religion and nationality" "has no other meaning than to deny Ahad Ha'am's right to cultural difference."[18] The bottom line is that, as Shumsky makes clear, the distinction of so-called political Zionism from so-called cultural Zionism is a false and ideological binary from poststate historiography.[19]

I wish once more to emphasize that I am not promoting a gentler, kinder version of Zionism. Any version of that program—whether statist or substate autonomy—involves and always involved grave appropriation of the territories of other peoples who already lived in Palestine and had done so for well over a millennium. Let us not forget that for all the appeal that Ahad Ha'am's sense of the value of cultural difference holds (at least for me), it involved as well the notion that "the constant renewal of Jewish life in the diaspora would be impossible without establishing a national center in Palestine."[20] No one was asking the Palestinians, the people who were already there. I am neither promoting nor apologizing for any form of Zionism. These visions of substate autonomies do point the way, however, to deterritorialized nationalisms and especially to nationalisms that are not founded on ethnic sovereignties, on national self-determination in the sense to which we have become accustomed. If we abandon—as both historicizable and deconstructible—the opposition between the political and cultural, we can see that the crux of the matter is the shift from nationalisms without mononational sovereignty to nationalisms that insist on the plot of land that belongs to one nation and in which all members of that nation would normatively and ideally live. In moving to a more complete characterization of the nationalism that I have in mind, a move out of the Zionist thought world is thus imperative. (Or do I, perhaps, mean mandatory?) The twoness or doubledness dubbed spiritual and material or cultural and political can be now productively shifted to a twoness on the material plane (the only plane that I recognize) of the life of the nation within itself, wherever it is, and the life of the nation in contact, even intimate contact, with other nations sharing the same space(s).

The notion of the culture nation, the *Kulturvolk*, provides promising food for thought. For Alexander von Humboldt, the German *Volk* was a *Kulturvolk*, not a naturally sovereign entity. Of course, he lived prior to the unification of Germany (which was never, of course, the unification of all German speakers—Herzl in Budapest and then Vienna was a German not longing to go "home" to Erfurt or Frankfurt or even Berlin), but neither did he conceive or dream of such a formation. I hold that one simply cannot interpret historical figures by assuming (or stipulating) that had they lived when nation-states were common, they would have joined that throng, as is done regularly for Theodor Herzl by Zionist historians. The fact is that he didn't advocate a nation-state in the modern sense of sovereignty for one nation in one state, but he and the preponderance of his fellow early Zionists did advocate for multinational states.

To come back then to Chatterjee's syllogism: "If the nation is an imagined community and if nations must also take the form of states, then our theoretical language must allow us to talk about community and state at the same time." Nations emphatically do *not* need to take the form of states, and they may very well be communities. It goes without saying that the two domains, one inward-facing to the life of the nation within and across states and one outward-facing to the shared life of the state, or perhaps to the lives of the other nations that share the state, will not leave each other untouched. It is this touchability that makes possible change within the nation, such that once-accepted practices like slavery, wife beating, and general gender/sex and racial oppressions might be overcome within the context of the nation. This touchability—in both of its senses—is not always as easy as those examples; such examples as circumcision and practices of animal slaughtering continue to be very difficult. As vital to *Judaïté* as these practices are, the ethical objections to them need to be somehow answered, and it is not always easy. Indeed, this is the major part of the cultural vitality of diaspora. The untouched and pristine—ethnic "cleansing," we say—are deadly fictions.

Dual Loyalties: Leon Pinsker and Stateless Zionism

Leon Pinsker (Yiddish: Yehudah Leib Pinsker; Russian: Lev Semyonovich Pinsker; 1821–91) was a physician, a Zionist pioneer and activist, and the founder and leader of the Hovevei Zion movement, also known as Hibbat Zion (Lovers of Zion). He wrote the classic early (some would say the first) manifesto of Zionism, *Autoemancipation*, and is considered in Israel and by Zionists the world over *the* progenitor, before Theodor Herzl, of the Zionist movement. If he can be shown to have had a nonstatist understanding of the Jewish nation and even a nonstatist vision of Jewish settlement in Palestine, a major chink in the armor of the notion that nation and state are always bound together will have been discovered. It seems significant, then, that his ideas have been seriously distorted in their uptake in later and current Zionist thinking in order to force them to fit with post–World War II versions of Zionist statism.

This point, too, has been well demonstrated by Dmitry Shumsky, who shows that Pinsker, that paragon of Zionist thinkers, never deemed a Jewish state desirable, but rather always and ever imagined a substate territory of Jewish self-determination in which national life could continue within the multinational state.[21] This inconvenient fact has been systematically suppressed in the Zionist historiography, which designates Pinsker as the forerunner of the sovereign Jewish nation-state.[22] Far from presaging the Jewish nation-state, or for that

matter one of Hungarians, Pinsker's "Zionist" thought envisions multinational states holding together substate national groups, the very
model that is today called "anti-Zionism."

Conventionally, in the hands of the dominant statist-Zionist paradigm of historiography, Pinsker—not unlike Herzl in this regard—is
deemed to have had an assimilationist period in his life and thought
and then, following a historical catastrophe, the wave of pogroms in
southern Russia in 1881, called at the time the "Storms in the South,"
to have had a conversion to nationalism, read as statism. Shumsky
definitively reveals this narrative to be a tendentious, anachronistic
legend. By reading Pinsker's Russian writings from before the supposed turn, a task that Shumsky is the first to take on, he establishes
that Pinsker's thought was not assimilationist before the so-called
Storms in the South, nor was it statist after them. Before the catastrophe in question, Pinsker had already written in the Russian-language
Jewish journal he founded, *Sion* (!), that the enlightened Jews of
a liberalizing Russia (at that time) "should aspire to the twin goals
that 'history had placed before them' at this time: 'to become the sons
of their time and their immediate homeland without ceasing to be'
true Jews."[23]

In Pinsker, we have neither the assimilative notions of the civil-
emancipatory trend of Jewish thinking—ascribed by Zionist histori-
ographers to Pinsker's youth—nor just the ethnic-national Jewish
trend that others find in him. Rather, "Pinsker calls upon the Jew to
become the faithful sons of the Russian state," but not nation, "without relinquishing their ethnic (or in his words 'tribal') and national
bonds—indeed, he himself used the word 'national'—as Jews."
Shumsky demonstrates that there actually are two Russian substan-
tives, one meaning the Russian nation and one meaning the Russian
state: *Russkiy* versus *russiiskiy*.[24] This doubled loyalty to Russia and
to the nonterritorial Jewish nation is a very significant, almost

paradoxical demand on the Jews that Pinsker advances, but it is exactly that paradox that characterizes my definition of diaspora. "Sons of" is not a dead metaphor in Russian but a very living one indeed, marking a connection as palpable as that of biological fathers and sons. The Jews are thus being afforded by Pinsker a doubled identity as well as doubled loyalties and a doubled cultural location and doubled practices, the very model of a modern diaspora that I espouse.[25] I would go just a bit beyond Pinsker to assert that a diasporic condition involves cultural creativity that is located both in the spatial environment in which a particular collective of Jews lives and at the same time in the transspatial environment of other collectives not in the same place or even in contiguous spaces.

Pinsker worked even before his alleged "turn" from assimilation to Jewish emancipation *against* the demand that the Jews abandon their historical national identity, language, and cultural practices, in direct opposition to the model that offered everything to individual Jews, nothing to the Jews. As Shumsky writes: "How was it possible, Pinsker wondered together with those minority voices [within the Hungarian national camp], that while the 1848 laws clearly implied the principle of equal rights for all the nationalities residing in Hungary, in the case of the Jews, who certainly constituted a singular nationality alongside the other nationalities, this principle was not recognized?" And Shumsky goes on to remark, "This query was by no means obvious at a time when the ideal of Jewish emancipation was linked to a perception of the Jews as a religious confession that lacked the characteristics not only of a separate and particularistic collective body, but also, certainly, of a nationality."[26]

The innovation of this earliest thinker whom we have come to call a Zionist is reassertion of the identity of the Jews as a nationality alongside other nationalities, such as Romani, Slovaks, Serbs, and Croats, within diaspora and not a negation of diaspora! Nothing is said here about nation-states; indeed, insofar as it is a critique of the Magyarization of Hungary (the doctrine that the Hungarian state belonged only to ethnic Magyars and all other ethnic groups were guests or invaders), Pinsker's thought stands starkly against the nation-state idea. Pinsker writes in the 1860s: "What if . . . the Hungarians [= Magyars] were to take advantage of their numerical superiority to declare that the existence of the Slovaks or the Germans amongst them was immediately harmful to them, and were they then to begin to exterminate them or expel them? . . . Do you, like the medieval inquisition, fail to understand that diversity is life?"

Diversity is life. Would that the Hungarians (or Israelis) were listening today! The bottom line here is that far from being the originator of the idea of the Jewish (or any other) nation-state, Pinsker is the original theoretician of the doubled location of the Jews as well as of other peoples—in short, of diasporism: "He sought to turn the Jew from a member of an obviously homeless people into a person with a dual home, like a Greek in Odessa or a Ukrainian in Moscow. This element of a 'dual homeland' was extremely important to Pinsker and to the Russian Jewish context of his post-*Autoemancipation!* perception." Such polities were always made up of folks, as sons of the state and sons of their nations, with dual—not necessarily incompatible, but dual—loyalties. The crux is that the two identifications call for different *kinds* of loyalties.

None of the early progenitors of the Zionist idea, from Leon Pinsker to Ahad Ha'am to Theodor Herzl, envisioned a Jewish state, but rather a Jewish autonomous national region within a state composed of other nations as well. The idea, explicitly stated by most of these early Zionist thinkers, was to provide a model multinational state, not a nation-state and certainly not a negation of the Diaspora. If even the Zionists, those most nationalist of Jews, whose solution to the Jewish

Question I reject, nonetheless were able so clearly to distinguish between nation and state, why does it now seem so impossible for so many of our contemporaries? In the next chapter the concept of the Jewish Diaspora Nation, the no-state solution, will be explored in some depth and breadth.

6

Diaspora Nation

The word "diaspora" entered the English language at a "moment of high nationalism," as anthropologist Engseng Ho puts it, during what historians call the long nineteenth century (1789–1914), and the conjunction has colored associations with "diaspora" ever since.[1] In that context, it came to mean an abnormal condition in contrast with the normal state of "national" groups as sovereign occupants of a territory. "Diaspora" in its modern, negative acceptation is thus a product of "the West." A further turn of the kaleidoscope away from this Western configuration offers different visions of the past and for the future.

Until now in modern thought, there have been two allegedly crucial factors for the identification of a "diaspora." The first is purportedly temporal and refers to an earlier past in which the nation was one and sovereign, a condition that was interrupted, leaving it now homeless, weak, and assailable. The second is spatial, offering a descriptive model in which there is now a situation of homeland versus diaspora. Homeland, once again, is imagined as an ideal, diaspora as deeply, profoundly, necessarily a defective condition. According to these views, this has led to the conclusion that diaspora is a pathology whose only cure is a nation-state, for the Jews as well as for other nations, and to the neo-Zionist mode of thinking known as "negation of the diaspora," the idea that not only must there be a sovereign state of the Jews, a Jewish state, but that all Jews ideally would move there.[2]

I seek to replace these negative conceptions of diaspora with one that sees diaspora as foundational to the character of Jewish existence and a source of its cultural and political vitality. Diaspora is not primarily an event in the past but an ongoing condition, a form of cultural national life in which nations may continue to exist, robustly, but the existence of and insistence on a piece of land that ideally incorporates only folks of that nation—and not only that, but all of them, or the vast majority of them—is simply not in play. This revision of the ideal has the consequence of more than one nation sharing the same land—Hungarians and Jews, for instance—and again betimes sharing the same government within the life of a diasporic nation such as the Jews.

The same people can, moreover, belong to more than one diaspora at the same time. For instance, there is the Sephardic Diaspora, whose members are thus at one and the same time members of the set of Jews and members of the subset of Sephardim. The young scholar Menashe Anzi has written of the structure of the Diaspora of the Yemenite Jews: "In addition to being part of a larger Jewish network, Yemenite Jewish migrants maintained many connections with Yemenite Muslim migrant communities in the Red Sea countries," and "the Yemenite Jewish diaspora also affected the lives of Yemenite Jews in Yemen."[3] This is virtually a model diaspora, disrupting such formulae as "the Jews of Israel and the Diaspora." There are also Ashkenazi Jews, who form a diaspora of their own.[4]

In the place of the nation-state, the no-state solution I offer is a diasporist vision for the future of the Jews doubly situated at home and abroad in their *doikayt*, their here and now. As I've noted before, this is a term drawn from the language of the Jewish Bund, the Yiddish socialist mass movement of pre–World War II Jews in Central and Eastern Europe. I adopt *doikayt* to denote commitment to the welfare of the people and their culture among whom one lives. A favorite Bundish slogan was "Dort vo ikh leb; dort is mayn Heym"—

"There where I live, there is my homeland." This Jewish commitment must be to fighting against oppression of all who are so oppressed, *where I live. Yiddishkayt* represents Jewish commitment to collectives in other places and perhaps other times to whom I am culturally and affectively bound, the Jews. To be sure, the use of the Yiddish term *Yiddishkayt* is itself problematic and even self-negating insofar as it seems to exclude the non-Yiddish-speaking Jews of the Global South, but that can be ameliorated somewhat with *Judaïté* and *Judezmo*.

These cultural and affective bonds, *Yiddishkayt, Judaïté, Judezmo,* are the cultural ties and commitments to other collectives that I identify as part of my nation living under other political formations or states.[5] The doubledness of diasporic identity opens a productive space for maintaining the value of this contradiction without jettisoning either mode of value.[6] Each of the poles can critique and inform the other, because both represent a great value and necessity for human flourishing. *Yiddishkayt/Judezmo/Judaïté* is an old-new mode of Jewish existence: Diaspora Nation.

Diaspora Nations

I offer two theses for this chapter: the general thesis that diaspora nationhood is not at all a special case or exceptional condition and the special theory that "the Jews" is a diaspora nation.

The Black Diaspora

Highly illuminating comparisons can be made to the usage of "diaspora" in the study of the cultural connections of people of African descent in the world.[7] A nice example of such a diaspora that we can observe being constructed in our time is the Black Diaspora. In the twentieth century, Martin Baumann writes, "long established 'Black communities' outside the African continent became renamed as diasporas. A unity of those once enslaved thus was and is constructed; a mythical relation of all overseas 'Blacks' with an idealized 'Africa' arose; and politically, former and present power relations were pointed out and questioned."[8]

One of the most important aspects of the history of African diaspora is that "Africa" is clearly and avowedly not a territory but a construct. African-descended people around the world did not come from a place called "Africa" but from Dahomey, the Cameroons, Ghana, Ivory Coast, Kenya, the Congo, and so on (some of these names are anachronistic), places of distinct historical and cultural identities. As the early twentieth-century founder of black study in America, W. E. B. Du Bois, famously wrote: "The idea of one Africa to unite the thought and ideals of all native peoples of the dark continent belongs to the twentieth century and stems naturally from the West Indies and the United States. Here various groups of Africans, quite separate in origin, became so united in experience and so exposed to the impact of new cultures that they began to think of Africa as one idea and one land."[9] What is important here is that the diaspora is produced in real time out of the narratives of a land of origin, whatever its objective status, as well as out of the current robust cultural connections sustained, in part, by that narrative. Going even further—and here only suggesting this—one might conclude that the homeland is produced by the diaspora.

Territory, to underline the point again, is not a necessary condition for the existence of a diaspora nation. Diaspora theorist Robin Cohen has even proposed that there are diasporas that are not characterized by connection to a "homeland," even an imaginary one, but are based rather on ties of solidarity with coethnics in other countries.[10] He refers to these formations as somewhat anomalous "deterritorialized diasporas." However, I see deterritorialized diaspora not as a special case or exceptional form of diaspora, but rather as its ideal type.

Diaspora is an ongoing cultural situation applicable to people who participate in a doubled cultural (and frequently linguistic) location in which they share a culture with the place in which they dwell, but also with at least one other group of people who live elsewhere, a situation in which they have a local and a translocal cultural identity and expression at the same time. To be diasporic calls for taking care of—not "boosting," "supporting," or being "proud of"—both your nation and the folks of your locale who are not members of your nation and striving for the productive and just life for both collectives.[11] This passion provides a base for other solidarities to emerge, but always concrete ones, not abstractions, engaging ardently with the nation, especially the transsovereign nation. Poland before World War II was an excellent example of a transsovereign nation in which the Polish nation lived partly in Germany, partly in the Ukraine, partly in Slovak territories, and even more, yet maintained a strong Polish cultural identity, even as they were participating in the political life of these different countries and governments.

None of this needs imply trauma, an original scene of forced dispersion, a longing for a homeland, or even the existence of a myth of one homeland. To put it concretely, it is not the Temple having been destroyed that constitutes the diaspora of Jewry, but the recitation all over the world of laments for the Temple on the exact same day and frequently with the exact same dirges. It is a condition that students of culture refer to as synchronic—that is, descriptive of a situation now in the present—not only diachronic, descriptive of events that happened in the past.

The *'Umma*

The Islamic *'umma* provides some other apt points of comparison here. Mobility, not stability in a place, is intrinsic to both the history and the norms of Islam. Islam does not begin with the birth of the

Prophet but with a displacement—the displacement of the early be-
lievers from Mecca to Medina. Abraham's "founding" of the People
also starts with a displacement from one place to another. Moreover,
every Muslim is required to make a pilgrimage journey to Mecca once
in their lifetime without any expectation of settling there. These jour-
neys globalize Islam, not least because they are sites of the sharing of
artistic practices that are thus doubly located in the local artistic
worlds of the different Muslim communities. Finally, as cultural historian of Islam Finbarr Flood formulates it, "The need to negotiate
between the local and the trans-local, the lived experience of the quo-
tidian and the ideal of the umma, an imagined community with a
global reach, has been a distinguishing figure of Islamic cultures from
their inception."[12]

Flood's use of the term "imagined community" here must be
taken seriously, because it is the preferred term among scholars today
to refer to the nation.[13] The ʾumma, a word frequently translated as
"nation," is very close in many of its decisive characteristics to the
Jewish ʾumma as well: ʾumma is the same word that Jewish Arab writers use to describe their people/peoplehood.[14] Obviously, a Muslim
ʾumma in a diaspora comprising Spaniards, Arabs, Persians, Chinese,
African Americans, and Indonesians is a diaspora that has come into
being through cultural and religious contacts, not one that has been,
traumatically or not, scattered from a putative homeland. Such coming into being does not discredit in the slightest the claim of a collective to be a nation, although it might trouble their claim to a national
homeland.[15]

There should be no mistake: Mecca is not the homeland that produces this diaspora, any more than there are connections with people
"back home." Mecca is the Holy City, and pilgrimage there is the
practice that enables the doubled location of the communities of
the ʾumma, including their shared artistic practices, which are then

located in two contexts and locations: the translocal Islamic one and the local traditions and conditions of artistic and other cultural practice.[16] Think, for instance, of Turkish and Persian Islamic art, what they share and how they differ, fed by contact with the artistic practices of Istanbul, on the one hand, and Isfahan, on the other, but also through contact with each other in Islamness through the communicative medium of the pilgrimage to Mecca. It is these doubled and shared practices that inspire me to refer to the 'umma as a diaspora.

But 'umma it is, and not a church, just as the Jews are an entity that exists by virtue of cultural connections (broadly speaking), an 'umma (or 'am), both words deriving from words for kinship and family.

The Shaping of Jewish Representation

The view of diaspora that I am offering here with respect to the Jewish folk has even more precise parallels among other human collectives. A wonderful case in point is the early and continuing diaspora of people from Hadramawt in Yemen across and around the Indian Ocean, a diaspora surprisingly like that of the Jews in many of their shared features. These are folks with deep and early ties, including of kinship with the Prophet Muhammed, and thus have special (not universally positive) status among Muslims. What is most important for my concern here is that they have spread quite widely and formed communities of their own around and even across the Indian Ocean over the last several centuries.

As Ho writes, showing how a diaspora—not the concept but the thing on the ground—functions, "The Adeni [a famous saint] was born in Tarim but died in Aden. It was at the place of death and burial that he became famous, the focus of pilgrimage and controversy. The same is true of those who followed him across the Indian Ocean. In all these cases, what is important is not where they were born but where they died and were buried. Seen in this way, the Adeni, his saintly colleagues, and their graves were not simply like a diaspora but indeed gave representational shape to one."[17]

I claim that there are three components that constitute the group of scattered Jewish collectives as a "diaspora," as one thing—hence the singular "the Jews"—that give representational shape and vitality (the opposite of atrophy) to that diaspora. They are a common narrative—even if a highly contested one—of "us," a common language that differentiates us from the other folks with whom we share space, a language that is itself perfectly diasporic in its hyphenations—Judeo-German, Judeo-Tajik, Judeo-Arabic, Yinglish—and a set of practices shared by "us" across time and space (sometimes shared even via rejection).[18] The most fecund and compelling versions of these representations still may ground them in theistic language, but, I contend, it ain't necessarily so.[19] What is necessary, in my understanding and view, is a depth and complexity of knowledge and experience that puts real flesh and bones on the name "Jew," not representing it as a matter of empty or virtually empty "pride."

The second and third of these are what I have been calling here, following Ho, "representations" of a national community and identity. Kwame Anthony Appiah, our prime example of an avowed cosmopolitan, considers these representations to be insufficient to found special ties to those folks of one's nation: "It could still be that special responsibilities make sense within truly thick relations (with lovers, family, friends) but not within the imaginary fraternity of our co-nationals."[20] According to Appiah, these "thick" relations are limited to the relations of parents to children, siblings, lovers, and the like, while such as "political, ethnic, or religious affiliations" are only imaginary and don't count. My argument is that it is the representations, the shared stories, the shared past—even if imagined—languages, modes of joking, practices on particular days and the like that add up to relations like those of lovers or siblings, that thicken the relations between people and produce a family-like sense of identification.

To recapitulate: this is a model that is very different from the cosmopolitan, almost its opposite. The cosmopolitan is a part of no collective, by definition, other than the collective of all humans, while the diasporic person is an impassioned member of at least two collectives. The cosmopolitan ideal seems always to end up with some version or another of the unmarked (universal) being as determined by whoever's in power, as we have seen in the discussion of Appiah in the introduction. The diasporic existence is taking care of your nation and working hard at some aspect(s) of its continuing cultural vitality and at the same time taking care of and with your neighbors in the here and now (especially oppressed neighbors) and striving for the productive and just life for both collectives. Doubled solidarity interrupts the tunnel vision that enables lack of concern for all other people than the ethnos while empowering at the same time passionate engagement on two fronts, the local cross-ethnic one and the translocal diasporic one.[21] This passion provides a base for other solidarities to emerge, but again, always concrete ones, not abstractions. Engaging ardently with the nation, especially the transsovereign nation (the nation spread over two or more sovereign states), may foster deep solidarity with others when it is diasporic in this sense.[22] Indeed, Césaire's "universal rich with all that is particular, rich with all the particulars there are, the deepening of each particular" requires that some collectives be ever deepening each particular to achieve that universal. National literatures must be studied and thought about in the context of world literature, and philology must not serve ethnocentrism or jingoism, racism, or anti-Semitism. But who's going to keep talmudic learning going, if Jews don't do it—a few Oxbridge dons and Alemannic professors? Who's going to continue Native American dance and language, who's going to keep Amazonian ontologies alive, if not folks from those nations—a few anthropologists? To put it another way: who will turn "the mass-graves of the forgotten," those very nearly buried products of historical Jewish creativity, into "enduring monuments" of those "remembered and cherished," to use Hannah Arendt's evocative language?[23] When seen from this perspective, diaspora nationalism can be grasped as the gift of any one and each collective to all of humanity.

The Unchosen People

It is the conjunction of narrative of ties of kinship with cultural ties of many kinds that short-circuits any attempt to impose a universalistic cosmopolitanism on a diasporic nation. The former are a matter of being born—or "naturalized" as converts—into that collective "the Jews"; the latter are the ways in which that collective represents itself and perpetuates itself, both to itself and to others, regardless of the exigencies of geographical location. What Ho says of the Hadrami Muslims is equally true of the Jews: "We are emboldened in calling these persons a society, in the singular, only because they share stories about themselves and each other, many noble, but not all complimentary."[24]

As I have argued, Jewishness is a statement not about the essence of a human being but just of genealogy, more analogous to being a member of a family, with all the problematics of family resemblances, than being a member of a political party or a philosophical school. You cannot choose your family of origin; you are born into that family, and similarly, one is born into Jewry. Of course, neither the state nor an autonomous community may enforce in any way that condition, except perhaps on children.[25] "Although tradition is unavoidable," writes political theorist Mark Bevir, "it is so as a starting point, not as something that determines, or even limits, later performances."[26] In modernity, being Jewish is an existential stance, phenomenological/ontological, but one that speaks strongly against the notion of the ontologically autonomous individual. That is because that being always already is social, and a continuity of representative practices—tradition—always already marks that being. As Bevir has clarified, "The concept of tradition captures an ontological fact or argument; that is, humans necessarily have their being in a social context which influences them."[27] We cannot, he argues, conceive of anyone holding beliefs or performing actions aside from that social context. "Everyone at all times sets out from an inherited set of shared understandings that is acquired during a process of socialisation."[28] "Just as we do not choose the language into which we are born, so do we not choose the tradition into which we are born and through which we are shaped as individuals."[29] As I have said above, we are thrown into the world Jews, to make of that what we will.

How we make of it an identity as a diasporic nation involves many other forms of representation, practices shared by us across time and space, centered on the Talmud and its language, a common linguistic culture in any language, not just Hebrew, that differentiates us from the other folks with whom we share space and local languages. The study of the discourses of the Talmud suffuses and informs all other Jewish social practices.

The Talmud as the Font of Living
Waters for *Judaïté*

The Talmud was produced in Diaspora. The Jews of Babylonia had been there for centuries, pursuing lives while maintaining some form of Judean identity, but without the Oral Torah and rabbinic literature.[30] Contact, however, having been maintained with the Jews of the Land of Israel, eventually the Mishna (actually very early in the history of that text) was brought to Babylonia, and a robust rabbinic culture of learning and teaching was instituted there via those contacts. The Babylonian Talmud is strongly assertive and productive of the profound value of diasporic Jewish learning and life.[31] The culture of learning became so vibrant in its new sites in the east that eventually a Talmud to rival the one of Palestine emerged, with its own local cultural contexts as well as the deep ties with the west (Palestine), and became by the eleventh century *the* dominant Talmud to the point that the Palestinian Talmud was nearly forgotten.[32] And so was born the Jewish Diaspora around the Talmud, a diaspora that was to sustain Jewish life for over a millennium—and counting.[33]

Every student of the Talmud knows after a while, without necessarily being able to articulate it, that the Talmud is not the book at the center of the commentaries; it is the whole thing—the process and the product too.[34] The very liveliness of the talmudic style, with almost any assertion rejected by some other authority within the text itself, produces a sense of the presence of the conversations, as if the reader were there when it happened. A great deal of that process is grounded in the notorious disputationality of the Talmud as well as in its practices of study and learning. Ideas are generated out of quotations, quotations contested, amended, emended, combined, and renewed.[35]

Thus, it is primarily not the talmudic text itself that gives it this power of life, this ability to generate life and liveliness, but the practices that surround the text, its study—usually in pairs or small groups—then the entry of its cadences and melodies, commonplaces and styles of speech into the daily speech of Jews everywhere.[36] The Talmud was considered not only or even primarily as a text, as a book, but as a set of practices, and these practices are quintessentially diasporic, even foundational for the Jewish Diaspora as a positive form of life, as opposed to a negative space of deprivation.[37]

Paul Mendes-Flohr of the University of Chicago Divinity School captures the sensibility of which I speak in his description of the idea of Martin Buber and Franz Rosenzweig's famous Jewish school for adults in Frankfurt, the Lehrhaus:

> Noting that as exemplified by the post-traditional library, one's cultural identity is constituted dialogically, Buber and Rosenzweig sought to re-center the intellectual horizons of culturally deracinated Jews in Talmud Torah, the classical mode of Jewish learning. Talmud Torah, they observed, is a form of dialogical study whereby Jews gather communally, generally in the synagogue, to engage in a conversation with sacred texts and their interpretations that have evolved over the millennia. So pursued, Talmud Torah attains a sacramental aura. Although Buber and Rosenzweig called on post-traditional Jews to engage anew in the dialogical tradition of Jewish learning, they acknowledged that those who would heed the call will invariably bring into the dialogue their multicultural, cosmopolitan sensibilities.[38]

I would emphasize only that surely Buber and Rosenzweig did not regret the invariability of the brought-into-the-dialogue multicultural (this usage is startlingly anachronistic) sensibilities but welcomed them, for as they understood well, such cultural hybridity is the very life blood of Jewish learning and especially its generator, the Talmud understood as a text, but also—and more significantly—as the communal practices of the study in all the forms that study took. For centuries now, the Babylonian Talmud has been generally regarded, by friend and foe alike, as the foundational document of what has come to be called Judaism. Talmudic study—its melodies, rhythms, and counterpoints—has been the music of Jewish existence, providing the background tunes for even the most everyday of Jewish lives, and the discourses of the Talmud suffuse and inform Jewish social practices. Available to the learned in multiple volumes with indices and concordances, commentaries and supercommentaries on those commentaries, they are also passed around in common talk, as pious homilies or ironic explanations as well, I might add, as folk stories and proverbs to the extent that the great historical linguist Max Weinreich referred to all of Jewish life (at least in Eastern Europe, but it need not be limited thus) as "the way of the Talmud" (*derekh hashas*), incorporating blessings and curses, foodways, the stock of proverbs that Jews employed, and, of course, not to be forgotten, the ritual practices and avoidances that characterize Jewish existence.[39]

It is the history of reception of the book that makes it worthy to be canonized. The commentaries on the text—even its critics—are what lend it the power and authority that make for a canonized text. The Talmud was not born canonical, it became so through the institutions and practices of learning, commenting, critiquing, and resolving difficulties that ensued through the centuries.[40] Moreover, it was those activities themselves that also created the form of life in which the Talmud was the soundscape for Jewish culture *tout court*. The product is the Diaspora Nation, as we will see more fully in the next chapter.

7

The Lullaby of Jewland

In a medieval Jewish legend preserved in *The Book of Tradition*, by Abraham Ibn Daud (1110–c. 1180), we can see both the influence of the study of Talmud on Jewish culture and the way it undergirds the existence of a diasporic nation. It is the story of a human collective that is widespread geographically, living in different places, but strongly and tightly joined together by the stories and by practices of the Talmud. Precisely because the story is entirely fictive, as its most recent editor and scholarly commentator, the late Gerson D. Cohen, has demonstrated, we can learn from it what its author was trying to tell us in making it up.

Muslim pirates capture a ship bearing four great Talmud scholars, R. Ḥushiel, the father of Rabbenu Ḥananel; R. Moses; R. Shemariah, the son of R. Elḥanan; and "as for the fourth," the narrator says, "I do not know his name." The three named rabbis are well-attested talmudic scholars and leaders of the Jewish world in the Middle Ages. They are "travelling from the city of Bari to a city called Sefastin . . . on their way to a Kallah convention." The destination city was made up, but the institution of the Kallah, a month-long mass Talmud study session, was very much real.[1]

Not having revealed to the commander of the pirate ship that they are important talmudic scholars, they are all redeemed individually by different Jewish communities in accord with the Mitzva to redeem captives: Rabbi Shemariah is sold in Alexandria and ends up in Fostat

(Cairo), where he becomes head of the academy in the place that eventually Maimonides would call home. Rabbi Ḥushiel is sold in Kairawan in Tunisia, where he begets his son Rabbenu Ḥananel, who wrote the first great commentary on the Talmud. Rabbi Moses ends up in Cordova, where he replaces the former dependence of that community on the Babylonian center with his own learning and teaching; they will neither depend on nor support the Babylonian academies, for now they have knowledge of the Babylonian book. After Moses demonstrated the inadequacy of the interpretation of the Talmud offered by their local Babylonian-trained rabbi, the latter, one "R. Nathan the judge walked out, and the litigants went after him. However, he said to them: 'I am no longer judge. This man, who is garbed in rags and is a stranger, is my master, and I shall be his disciple from this day on. You ought to appoint him judge of the community of Cordova.' And that is exactly what they did. The community then assigned him a large stipend and honored him with costly garments and a carriage. . . . The King [of Andalucia] was delighted by the fact that the Jews of his domain no longer had need of the people of Babylonia."

Gerson Cohen points out that this narrative represents a new beginning, the beginning of a new episteme in Jewish life, by indicating a crucial point in this narrative: "In the whole history of Jewish oral tradition, which is the prime subject of Ibn Daud's tract, these four scholars were the only ones, with the exception of the first Moses, who had not 'received' their authority from a recognized predecessor." The entire mode of authority has shifted: "What Ibn Daud wants to tell us is that R. Moses' arrival in Spain—and of R. Hushiel in Qairawan and of R. Shemariah in Cairo—marks the transition to a new era in Jewish learning, the era of the Rabbinate. The arrival of the 'four' captives in their respective new homes spells the end of the Gaonate and hegemony of Babylonia and, on the other hand, the beginning of learning the world over." That is, the fundamental conditions and place of scholarship within the Jewish world is now disseminated throughout the world.

The Jewish communities that previously had been mere dependents on the central authority in Babylonia now were independent centers of learning and deeply connected with each other via that means. At the same time, even their forms of talmudic study were powerfully influenced by the modes of thought in the differing Arabic and European-Latin worlds in which they dwelled. What had been previously invested in transmission from the central authorities to relatively ignorant Jews in the peripheries, Ibn Daud is saying, is now invested in book learning, with the sharp emphasis on the learning shared and produced among the different geographically spread collectives of Jews, and it is this cultural connection via the book that constitutes the Talmud as diaspora.

The narrative composed by Ibn Daud seems to have been a rewriting of a much earlier legend according to which these communities had been founded by Jews shipped off from Palestine by the Roman emperor Vespasian. Ibn Daud's version, which became very well known throughout the Jewish world, is thus a revision of the concept of diaspora from a disaster to a space of vibrant Jewish life, the vehicle of which is the shared practice of study of Talmud.[2] Now the book is the homeland. It was at this time, sometime around the eleventh century, that the Jews became the People of the Talmud, a diasporic nation joined by the study of the Talmud and a multitude of related practices.

Ibn Daud's story revolves around leaders of that nation, elite interpreters of the Talmud, but as R. Nathan's ceding of his position to a man in rags shows, not all elites are elitist. A somewhat complicated Jewish joke might help to illustrate these themes. Here's one version:

A rabbi and a cantor are standing in the largely empty synagogue one day, talking mystically about how, given the awesome glory of God's Infinite Divine Presence, they are each really "nothing." "Yes," says the rabbi, "I am nothing!" The cantor also affirms, looking up to the heavens, "O God, I am completely nothing!" And they go on like this for several rounds—"I am nothing. . . . I am utterly nothing."

Meanwhile, the synagogue's janitor is off in the corner on his hands and knees, scrubbing the floor. Filled with humble devotion, he has all the while been repeating in a gentle voice, "O Lord, You are everything and I am nothing. . . . I am nothing." The rabbi and cantor at one point bend their ears to listen and, after a few moments, come to realize what the lowly janitor is saying. At this, the rabbi nudges the cantor and smugly says, "Look who thinks he's nothing!"[3]

This joke, which mocks the pseudo-humility of elites in the face of the true humility of a member of the working class, is itself drawn from the world of talmudic learning. In the Talmud, Berachos 34a, we find a statement that one genuflects at the beginning and the end of certain blessings in the daily liturgy, and the Talmud informs us that if someone wishes to genuflect on more occasions, we stop them. The thirteenth-century commentators known as Tosfos then ask: And if he wants to genuflect, why not let him? (After all, it is out of piety and humility that he wishes to genuflect.) To which the answer comes that this self-humiliation will cause pride in him.

The Talmud, Yiddish, and the
Diaspora Nation

That joke about the pride of the humble is just one way in which the high discourse of the Talmud has entered into the world of every-day discourse of Jews through various cultural means—through story, humor, song, and even through the effect of Talmud study on the languages of the Diaspora itself.

The study of Talmud, shared throughout the communities of Israel, produced and maintained shared narratives, forms of speech and writing, practices, proverbs, and the like that sustained and maintained the communities as a diaspora, as a single thing. The study of the Talmud is generative as well of shared linguistic styles—for instance, the habit of answering a question with a question, the rhythms of Jewish speech—that most powerfully generate Diaspora.[4] This discursive tradition emerged from the tradition of *lernen*, the study of Talmud and discourse about such study, shared in the many spaces in which Jews, learned and less learned, gathered together. For deeper understandings we reach for comparisons, here with black study.

One of the most incisive explorers of blackness today is Fred Moten, who writes:

Can this sharing of a life in homelessness, this interplay of the refusal of what has been refused and consent, this undercommon appositionality, be a place from which to know, a place out of which emerges neither self-consciousness nor knowledge of the other but an improvisation that proceeds from somewhere on the other side of an unasked question? ["unasked—the question of the meaning of (black) being, the question of the meaning of (black) things."] But not simply to be among one's own; rather, also, to live among one's own in dispossession, to live among the ones who cannot own, the ones who have nothing and who, in having nothing, have everything.[5]

Notice how close Moten is here to Rosenzweig as discussed in the previous chapter. "Sharing a life in homelessness," as Moten describes black sociality, is the very definition of diaspora as I have been re(en)-visioning that term and concept. By the somewhat overegged "under-common appositionality," I, at any rate, understand Moten to be articulating the desire to be both an accepted part of the commons and also to refuse that, almost exactly the dilemma of many modern Jews, perhaps of modern Jewry. The refusal of home is the refusal of physical home, living "among one's own in dispossession." By having "nothing," no state, no home, no sovereign possession, the people may have everything, as Rosenzweig insisted in his anti-Zionism.

The sounds of talmudic tradition, a practice of reading and riff-ing, chanting and improvising, are also quite clearly in the realm of Moten's sense of "chant and koan and moan and *Sprechgesang*, and babble and gobbledygook, le petit nègre, . . . pidgin, baby talk, bird talk, Bird's talk, bard talk, bar talk, our locomotive bar walk and black chant, our pallet cries and shipped whispers, our black notes and black cant, the tenor's irruptive habitation of the vehicle, the monas-tic preparation of a more than three-dimensional transcript, an imagi-nal manuscript we touch upon the walls and one another, so we can enter into the hold we're in, where there is no way we were or are."[6] It is the Talmud that produces the sounds of diasporic Jewish sociality, just as jazz produces, as Moten shows, black sociality.[7] The institu-tions and practices of learning, commenting, critiquing, and resolving difficulties that ensued through the centuries as the Talmud became canonical created the form of life in which the Talmud was the sound-scape for Jewish culture and thus Jewish worldwide sociality. The study of Talmud has been and still is an immersive experience (to use a current neologism), so immersive as to generate a culture. Despite its shady reputation in certain circles for belonging only to elites, the Talmud, its melodies and rhythms, its questioning tone—indeed, its querulousness—that is Jewish jazz.

I want to say here again as clearly as I possibly can: I am not seeking or proposing here in any of this discourse of mine an analogy of black pain to Jewish pain. I have instinctively felt always that these analogies were somehow complicit with the racist status quo.[8] What I am seeking is connection and learning at the places at which I think I can learn something, certain points of comparison—or yes, I even confess—local analogy where the juxtaposition seems to me illuminating for my claims, my possibilities of understanding something, where I can learn something about *Judaïté* from black theory.

This Jewish jazz has engendered Jewish languages as well. Those rhythms, melodies, intonations have given rise to Yiddish, *Judezmo*, and a dozen or more other Jewish languages. At least Yiddish, moreover, has been disdainfully referred to as *zhargon* (= jargon, accent on the final syllable), which we might imagine the European equivalent of the English term *pidgin*: " 'The most magnificent drama of the last thousand years of human history' was not enacted with its strophes and prosody ready-made.[9] It created a new speech. A combination of, first, nautical English; second, the 'sabir' of the Mediterranean; third, the hermetic-like cant talk of the 'underworld'; and fourth, West African grammatical construction, produced the 'pidgin English' that became in the tumultuous years of the slave trade the language of the African coast."[10] With just a few substitutions of terms, Moten could be describing the origins of Yiddish from German, Hebrew, Slavic languages, and a solid injection of the language and language patterns of the Talmud itself and talmudic *lernen*, as well as Odessan horse thieves. Both Yiddish and West African have the potentials for resistance to different forms of colonial cultural hegemony; as Moten writes, "The experiment is poetic; {pidgin} [zhargón] is a poetics."[11]

Certain elements within German Jewry condemned the Jewish jargon of Central and Eastern Europe. "Little Jews" (*Mauschel* or *Moishele*) could not speak, allegedly were not capable of speaking, a

real language such as *Hochdeutsch* until a Jewish savant of the eighteenth century, Moses Mendelssohn, set out to teach Moishele how.[12]
Mendelssohn, moreover, while remaining "orthodox" in his *Judaïtude*,
nonetheless rejected talmudic learning, with all of the various trap-
pings of *Mauscheln* that it produces. And we must not forget that it
was Jews, such as Herzl, the founder of the Zionist movement, who
circulated and popularized the derisive term *Mauscheln* (Moses-talk)
for Yiddish-inflected German speech by Jews.

The desire of Mendelssohn and Herzl for proper German, a desire subtended by a kind of internalization of anti-Semitism, parallels
Fanon's elegant and searching explanation of the desire of blacks for
"correct" speech.[13] Retelling a story in which a black teacher, Achille
from Martinique, is spoken to in pidgin by a white priest and answers
in perfect French, Fanon shows that the rejection of pidgin in favor of
the language of the colonizer is to avoid such infantilizing and hu-
miliating encounters. But Moten gently reproves: "The violence of
insincere and unflattering imitation that materializes such absence of
reflection [the internalization of the priest's contempt] is vividly portrayed in Fanon's text. However, infantilization of the ones who utter
the speech that, according to Fanon, cannot be spoken, does not
mean that the new speech is merely infantile."[14]

Moten enables yet another modulation toward a resolution of this
discussion here. He writes: "Fanon is concerned with the narcissism
of the new returnee, the social climber, as he or she links up with Arendt's own stringent analysis of the parvenu."[15] Arendt is one of the
classic instances of the category of the "anti-anti-Semite," of the Jewish variety, to be sure, the one who both blames the Jews, as it were,
for anti-Semitism and also essentially wills the Jews out of political
and epistemic existence in order to disappear anti-Semitism.[16] (It
must be said, however, that Arendt is an extremely complex figure, an
anti-Zionist who apparently donated money to Meir Kahana and the

Jewish Defense League when it was a local New York vigilante Jewish group. This can be explained, and needs to be, for it is precisely one possibility for anti-Zionism to be militant about Jewish defense in the Diaspora, and this was before Kahana's own turn to Zionofascism, but it certainly complicates the categorization of her as anti-anti-Semite.) Similarly. Fanon, in his writing on the "returnees," according to Moten, is a sort of anti-anti-racist.

Talmudic study—its melodies, rhythms, and counterpoints—has been the music of Jewish existence, the lullaby of Jewland. The study of Talmud is frequently literally musical, or even musicological. It provides the soundscape, the music of Jewish life.[17] In making this statement, I am shifting from thinking of the Talmud primarily as text so much as an oral and aural practice in and for itself, as have others.[18] As linguist Zelda Kahan Newman has shown, the intonation patterns of the Talmud are what make Yiddish sound "Jewish."[19] These particular patterns of intonation and the way they semantically match patterns in Yiddish were discovered—as noted by Newman—by Uriel Weinreich, and they are in no way "elitist" in Yiddish. And this nearly melodic speech pattern is by no means endemic only to Ashkenazic Jews or Yiddish speakers. Newman also documents the fact that according to Rav Kafih, intellectual leader of the Yemenite Jews in Israel, these patterns are found widely in the daily speech (in Judeo-Arabic) of his folk, too.

The study of Talmud could constitute the Jewish Diaspora both in antiquity and today because it provided a common language.[20] Jews have always had a separate language, or more precisely a set of separate languages, that marked them off as a nation alongside or even within other nations. Once there was Yiddish for the large majority of the world's Jews, and *Judezmo*, Judeo-Arabic (in all its varieties), Judeo-Persian, Judeo-neo-Aramaic, Judeo-Tajik (and others) for the rest. Now, most of these are gone from the world, or nearly so. I am persuaded that it is the very fact of a differentiated language that contributed mightily to the continued existence of the nation as such and that was critical in the formation of diaspora in the sense in which I use it in my thinking. Two questions arise then. The first is how did such a linguistic diversity constitute—or better, contribute to constituting—all Jews as a single collective? And second, how can we imagine this in a world in which many, perhaps most, Jews no longer share a Jewish language, unless that language is Hebrew?[21]

When I was a child, my parents spoke a language they called "Jewish"—translating the word "Yiddish" into English—when they didn't want children to understand. I once asked them if a certain person who worked for them spoke "Christian"; they didn't understand the question. The closest thing to "Christian" as a language is the medieval and early modern Jewish name for Latin, *galakhut/galakhes* (= tonsure talk, or *Monkish*). But Jews everywhere have had their own forms of speech.[22] Famously, according to the Midrash Leviticus Rabbah, one of the reasons that the Israelites were redeemed from Egypt is that they did not change their language. It was the fact of continued speaking Yehudit or Ivrit that enabled the collective to be preserved for the centuries in order that they would maintain a distinct identity upon being afforded the opportunity to leave Egypt. The eighteenth-century leader (perhaps inventor) of what is inaptly called today "ultra-orthodox" Judaism, the Hatam Sofer (1762–1839), realized well that the best guarantor of continued Judaic existence was continued speech in the Jewish language; in his time and place, of course, that was Yiddish. At the other end of Jewish modernity, Leon Trotsky (Lev Davidovich Bronstein) wrote, "The Jews of different countries have created their press and developed the Yiddish language as an instrument adapted to modern-culture. One must therefore reckon with the fact that the Jewish nation will maintain itself for an entire epoch to come."[23] He couldn't, of course, have foretold the Nazis.

Obviously these Israelites also must have spoken the language of Egypt—if only to receive their marching orders. (And what did Moses speak with his adoptive mother and her father? Or Joseph at the court?) The net result is the sort of diglossia typical of Jewish historical existence everywhere: a fluent, rich, complete Jewish language (*Yiddishkayt/Judezmo*) together with facility and participation in the language of the place (*doikayt*). Within the Diaspora context, it is the sharing of the Jewish tongue that provides the glue binding the dispersed, transnational nation into a collective, not simplex, but duplex, at the least.[24]

We can thus see (following Max Weinreich) that what conjoins all of the Judeo-languages is not the component that joins them to the languages of the locale in which they have come into being (Central Europe for Yiddish, and so on), but the component that is drawn from the shared language of the Jews, namely, the language of the Babylonian Talmud, already a rich amalgam of Hebrew and Aramaic. It is this component of Yiddish (and, I warrant, all other Jewish languages) that provides the vehicle for the cultural nexus that we name the Jewish Nation. In a profound sense, it is this/these Jewish language(s) that produce the shared soundscape of the world Jewish Diaspora—the deep structure for my seemingly ungrammatical question, "What is the Jews?" It is the shared components of these languages with the languages of the people that Jews live among that constitute them as diasporic, an irreducible component that is shared with the local population as well: Diaspora *loshn*.

From Talmud to Folk Song: *May ko mashme-lon*

Consider a famous Yiddish art song that became, among other things, a Yiddish and Hebrew folk song. It's by Avrom Reyzen (1876–1953). I first heard this song when I was about eight or nine years old.

I am giving here only one stanza in Yiddish transliteration and in my first stab at English to illustrate my point.[25]

> May ko mashme-lon der regn?
> Vos zhe lozt er mir tsu hern?
> Zayne tropns oyf di shoybn
> kayklen zikh vi tribe trern.
> Un di shtivl iz tserisn,
> Un es vert in gas a blote;
> Bald vet oykh der vinter kumen—
> Kh'hob keyn vareme kapote.

> What does the rain mean?
> What does it teach me?
> Its drops roll down the windowpane
> like sad tears.
> And my boots are torn,
> and there's mud in the street.
> Soon the winter will be here,
> and I don't have a warm coat.

I want now actually to talk the poem into English before giving an amended translation toward the end of this reading of it. The first and key phrase that generates the whole poem is *May ko mashme-lon*, which is drawn directly from the Aramaic of the Talmud, *Gemoro loshn*, where it literally means: "What does this teach us?" It is evoked when a given sentence quoted in the Talmud seems not to add anything to our knowledge, either because we know what it says already or because what it says seems trivial, a mere historical datum, a fact of no significance. Reyzen follows the Aramaic with a literal translation into Yiddish using the precise Yiddish idiom, which is itself a direct translation from the original Aramaic talmudic phrase: *Mai ko mashma lon*, which means literally "What does it make us hear?" but idiomatically "What does it teach us?" In other words, a Yiddish idiom based on a literal loan translation from Aramaic is used here to illuminate precisely the Aramaic phrase. As if the Aramaic one is taken from the Yiddish: in both "What does it make us hear?" means "What does it teach us?"

The answer to this question in the Talmud always discovers some normative reason for the statement having been made. Let's see now, then, a real example of this from the Talmud itself:

The Talmud relates that **Binyamin the shepherd ate bread and** afterward **recited** in Aramaic: **Blessed is the Master of this bread.** Rav **said,** he thereby **fulfilled** his obligation to recite a blessing. The Gemara objects: **But didn't** Rav himself **say: Any blessing that does not contain mention of God's name is not** considered a **blessing?** And there is no mention of God's name in the shepherd's blessing, so Rav seems to be contradicting himself. The Talmud then emends the formula of his blessing. **He said: Blessed is the All-Merciful, Master of this bread.** And "the All-Merciful" is indeed one of the names of G-d.

The Talmud asks: **But don't we require three blessings** in Grace after Meals? How did the shepherd fulfill his obligation with one sentence? The Talmud explains: **What is: fulfills his obligation, that** Rav **also said? He fulfills** the obligation **of the first** of the three **blessings,** and must recite two more to fulfill his obligation completely.

The Talmud asks: *Mai ko mashma lon?!* **What is he teaching us?** Once we've emended it in this way it seems that Rav's statement has no meaning; it doesn't add anything to what we already know. The Talmud answers: **Although he recited** the blessing **in a secular language,** other than Hebrew, as in the Aramaic that the shepherd used, he fulfilled his obligation. [Berakhot 40b][26]

Mai ko mashma lon, as we see, is a very technical term in the so-called elite discipline of talmudic study, but it escapes from that milieu into the world, from the world of *lernen* to the world of everyday human life in the present and hardly the life of only an elite.[27]

In the Yiddish poem, this common talmudic phrase isn't talking about a passage from the Mishna or a statement of the great Rav; it's talking about rain and the misery it brings to the poor Yeshiva *bokher*. The phrase itself breaks out from the House of Study and moves into the street, a perfect figure for the way that talmudic lingo functions in the generation of a whole—nonelite—culture.[28] Instead of "What does he teach us?" it comes to signify "What does it mean?" From the book to the mud! The thematization of the move from scholastic elite to the world of all Jewish life is matched by the enactment of it in the migration of the phrase from one *Sitz im Leben* to another, from the talmudic page to the suffering of poor Talmud scholars and the passionate interrogation "What does it teach us?" Just as any statement in the Talmud must teach us something, something significant, so also the miserable rain has to teach us something. With its translation from the Talmud's Aramaic used directly in more learned levels of Yiddish to a loan translation used in others, the poem is thus enacting, once again, and on this level also, the way that *Gemoro loshn* (Talmud lingo) enters into the everyday speech of Yiddish in all registers. Without recognition of the talmudic phrase—even if one has never actually learned a page of Talmud—the song is unintelligible, so the song functions also as a mode of education for the masses. Jewish language functions analogously to the illuminated windows of the great cathedrals in bringing the talmudic culture to Everyjew. As put by Frantz Fanon, "To speak means being able to use a certain syntax and possessing the morphology of such and such a language, but it means above all assuming a culture and bearing the weight of a civilization."[29]

This is how the first verse of the song would read *correctly* translated into English:

> Mai ko mashma lon the rain?
> What does it teach us?
> Its drops roll down the windowpane like sad tears.
> And my boots are torn
> and there's mud in the street.
> Soon the winter will be here,
> and I have not a warm coat.[30]

Gemoro loshn comes into the vernacular because the phrase is so pervasive in the mind of the Talmud students that it, and a version of the thought carried with it, goes out into the world and into Yiddish and articulates his misery. What does this misery mean? What is it teaching us? *Mai ko mashma lon?* Rain and cold have become a text to be read, to be interpreted, but absolutely retain their miserable concrete reality.

The last verse of the song is to my mind the most poignant of all:

> May ko mashme-lon mayn lebn?
> Vos zhe lozt es mikh tsu hern?
> Foyln, velkn in der yugnt,
> Far der tsayt fareltert vern.
> Esn teg un shlingen trern,

Shlofn oyf dem foist, dem hartn,
Teytn do di oylem haze—Un oyf oylem habe vartn.

Mai ko mashma lon my life?
What does it teach us?
Our youth is rotten and withered,
And we become old before our time.
We eat at others' tables and wash it down with tears.
My fist is my pillow,
We slay here This World
And await only the Next.[31]

The lament of the Yeshiva *bokher* turns finally into a cry of protest at his lot. The answer to the question What does it teach us, what does it give us to understand? is finally given: Nothing! The youths spend their lives in the dark House of Study growing old before their time without any of the pleasures of "This World"—not food, because they eat only the poor food that they are given. The Talmud itself defines its acolytes as "killing themselves in the Tent of Torah." Eating "days" (*Teg* in Yiddish) was the custom by which the Jewish villages supported the Yeshiva boys: Monday, I eat by Goldwasser; Tuesday by the Hazan's house, and so on. No wine, maybe no water even to drink; the poor food is washed down with tears. "Bread with salt you will eat" in order to be a Talmud scholar, "and on the ground you will sleep," intones the Mishna. *Gefilte fisch* and Moscat only in the next world.

It is important to claim and to underline the claim that this poem/song is not parodic, nor is it a "secular" attack on the tradition of study: it is a *cri de coeur* voiced from within. And the cry of the yeshiva *bokher* was successfully answered in the foundation of the great Yeshivos of the early twentieth century in which the *bokherim* did not suffer from cold or hunger or the humiliation of eating at others' tables, but were furnished with dormitories and dining facilities. It is the poem/song's blended language, manifesting the voice of bitter grievance from within, from within the language, from within the very idiom and melody of what is being grieved against, that makes it so powerful, a cry of pain, not of contempt, but also a stand *against* nostalgia, idealization, and romanticization.[32]

It is the recognition of that phrase, that formulaic question, as talmudic that is key to perceiving the power of Reyzen's poem. Although there is still much that could be said in a proper slow reading of the poem, one thing that must be mentioned here is that the melody with which the poem has been supplied and in which it is sung also evokes powerfully the melody of Talmud study. This is an excellent example in literary form of what Sarah Bunin Benor calls, with reference to various Jewish languages, the "transfer of Hebrew and Aramaic loanwords from rabbinic texts to the study of those texts and then to everyday speech."[33] Once again, the match between the thematization and the enactment of this linguistic element is a nearly perfect fit, because by entering the world of the art song, which is for Yiddish a direct track to folk song, the move of the phrase into the vernacular is not only described but performed. It is the sum total of such performances that, to my mind, constructs the language—in this case, Yiddish—as a Jewish language and thus a vehicle of Diaspora. It "works" as well in English, but for a much more limited segment of the population; in English, it will make sense only among those for whom the talmudic phrase is (still) a household word. To keep Jewish alive, we need many, many more such households.

The Elite and the Folk

It is clear from this discussion that without the energetic devotion to the literature of the Jews, and especially without the *lernen* of Talmud, the culture will indeed atrophy, and that culture is the

Diaspora. Benor records a list of Judeo-English phrases used by non-Orthodox—but highly engaged Jews—in California:

1. "These are machlekot leshem shamayim [debates for their own sake / for God's sake]."
2. "It doesn't matter—it's bediavad [after the fact] now."
3. "We have to restructure it so we get a nafka mina [practical outcome]."
4. "If you're going, then kal vachomer [all the more so] I should go." Any Jew who uses sentences like these either engages in traditional text study or (as is the case with many Orthodox women) spends time with people who do.[34]

It is hard but wonderful work to keep this kind of language going—the language, in all of its variations, that produces continuing Jewish creativity and the ever-new production of Jewish culture across time and space. Keeping a culture alive demands great effort, effort that is pleasurable for many. And there are levels and hierarchies. Those who study Talmud serve as teachers, formally and informally, for the Jews with whom they are in contact. Increasingly, those Jewish elites include women and are beginning as well to incorporate more radical resisters of the gendering of Jewish practice and learning, informal and formal; there are now radical queer Yeshivos in the world. But pains must be taken by many if they are to have an impact on learning. There's nothing unusual in that. What, after all, would happen, for instance, to the culture of European art music if nearly everyone in the world decided that it was just not worth the trouble to learn to play the piano well enough to play Beethoven's Hammerklavier sonata or to lern [sic] how to make sounds like the sound of Miles Davis on *Kind of Blue*?

A Language for Jewland: Some Thoughts, but No Resolution

Strangely, the two bases/substrates upon which I could imagine such a language developing (and which already exist) are Hebrew and English, but a very special Hebrew and a very special English, which we might name Judeo-Hebrew (or, somewhat more decorously, World Hebrew) and the language colloquially known as Yinglish, Yeshivish, or sometimes Frumspeak. I am dead serious. There is no reason why something like the processes that produced hyphenated Judeo-languages in the past could not occur again. As Benor has demonstrated, "Jewish American English exhibits most of the features common among diaspora Jewish languages."[35] After noting that there are important differences as well, she concludes: "These differences are significant enough that many scholars and lay people do not consider Jewish American English and premodern Jewish languages to be in the same analytical category. This understanding is related to the sense that historical events of the eighteenth to twentieth centuries represented a major earthquake in Jewish history, virtually destroying traditional cultural practices in Diaspora communities around the world." She argues that "the earthquake may not have led to complete destruction or, to extend the metaphor, that contemporary Jews are using much of the original blueprints as they rebuild their own cultural structures."[36] So it's not so far-fetched that a distinctive form of Jewish English could become the vehicle of world Jewish diasporic culture, especially since English is almost universally known around the world.[37]

At the same time, Hebrew is gradually becoming the shared language of greater and greater segments of world Jewry. This is, to be sure, largely a knock-on effect of state Zionism. The reason that more and more Jews speak Hebrew is because they have been in Israel for a time. Nonetheless, it seems that even bad causes can lead to good effects—at least sometimes. The possibility and promise of a World Hebrew as a shared first or second language for a large segment of Jewry provides one of the engines for a new diaspora.

What needs to be altered is the situation pointed out by Benor: "The existence of the State of Israel has changed the meaning of Hebrew writing in the Diaspora. Now writing in Hebrew is seen as an act of cultural connection to contemporary Israel, rather than connection to local, international, and historical Jews."[38] This orientation has to be resisted if Hebrew is to serve as a vehicle for the cultural connectedness of Jews and Jewish communities around the world, and I am surely not the only thinker to have made this point. We must recover Hebrew as a *Jewish* language, not only the Israeli language. This shift will involve a change in the very nature of the Hebrew that we write and speak around the world, because it is vital that it serve as a Jewish language, not an Israeli language. There is no reason to exclude the Jews of Palestine from participation in the old-new Jewish Diaspora.

The Rites of Return: Language beyond and before Language

Language is vital, but not the be-all and end-all of my imaginings. This brings us now to the question of shared cultural practices beyond language—to "doings" and things, material objects. Of highly prominent early Israeli historian Ben Zion Dinur, a recent commentator has observed: "He perceived that historical consciousness is not confined to literary practices only, but is encoded in folk culture, customs and ceremonies."[39] Dinur, a vital figure in the foundation of the educational system of modern Israel, made this judgment with respect to the construction of the nation-state, but these practices and the role they play are just as applicable to a diasporic nation, perhaps even more so. The holidays, the material culture—melodies for the liturgy, shofar, lulov and esrog for Sukkos, the Sukka itself, matza (but also chulent and lox and bagels)—all create a shared cultural world that, subsisting alongside of the local cultural world—and interacting with it—produces the doubled culture that marks diaspora, in this case the Jewish Diaspora Nation.

8

What Was I Thinking?

> I never felt the need to simplify myself or to create an artificial unity
> by way of denial; I accept my [cultural] complexity and hope to be
> an even more multifarious unity than I am now aware of being.
>
> *Gustav Landauer*

In this nonfinale, I am going to attempt an answer to the question posed in its title, a question frequently addressed to me, irenically or ironically and sometimes irately: What were you thinking?!

I am going to bring this book to a close (if not closure) where I began, by bucking the all too common proposition that the only mode of ethical Jewish existence in the present and future is essentially simply to disappear as a collective. This form of opposition to Jewish collective existence has been discussed at length and powerfully contested in a very important recent book by El'ad Lapidot of the University of Lille, to whose work I return here.[1] At first glance, this form of antagonism to "the Jews"—anti-anti-Semitism—seems more benign than others, in that it is generated out of the fight against anti-Semitism. Lapidot's fascinating book indicts this discourse of opposition to anti-Semitism—"anti-anti-Semitism"—for tacitly but essentially claiming that *any* statement about Jews or Jewish is ipso facto anti-Semitic: "Anti-anti-Semitism fundamentally rejects anti-Semitic knowledge of the Jewish: as mere perception, construction, projec-

tion, imagination, fantasy, and myth. . . . Anti-anti-Semitism most
fundamentally tends to criticize anti-Semitism not for thinking
against Jews, but for thinking of Jews at all, namely for engaging Jews
as an object of thought, as an epistemic entity."[2] Along with Lapidot,
I, too, totally reject the proposition that there is nothing to be said
about Jews; what there is to say is that there *are* Jews and historically/
existentially, we have made something of that, something perceptible,
graspable, and evaluable.[3]

It has been my experience for quite a long time that anti-Semites
(or anti-Jews) frequently do perceive important generalizations to be
made about Jews; they just get their values upside down. Thus, I have
based much of my work on *accepting* the premise of the "carnality" of
Jews and seeking to understand it as a virtue, not a vice. Therefore,
following Lapidot's lead provides a lucid and (for me, at least) compelling account of how the modern/postmodern account of "the
Jews" as a figment of the anti-Semites' discourse paradoxically ends up
complicit with anti-Semitism itself.[4]

In contrast to the thinkers of anti-anti-Semitism, this manifesto is
dedicated to making the Jews appear. The new Jewish Question is not
to be answered or made to go away, but to be ever put and ever con-
templated and disputed—the very office of the Jews in the world. The
Jewish Question, in my thinking, is indeed "What is the Jews?" Or as
Lapidot headily phrases it: "Put differently, anti-Semitism may be said
to be *necessarily* based on certain—problematic and partial as it may
be, but nonetheless—knowledge of Jews."[5] This is a total, absolutely
total, antithesis to the vision of Adorno and Horkheimer, on the one
hand, that the "Jew" of anti-Semites is solely a projection of their own
pathology and has nothing to do with "real Jews," whether living or
not and, on the other hand, the even more extreme version of Sartre
that even real and living Jews exist as such only by virtue of the anti-
Semitic *imaginaire*.[6] As I have been thinking for a long, long time,

many anti-Semites (especially the smart ones, such as Augustine and Kant) do perceive something real, if not complete, about Jews, especially our commitment to the flesh and the literal as emblematized in circumcision of the penis (not the heart). And, as I have argued too, they, such as Augustine and Kant again, just get the values upside down.[7]

I have striven to recover here some measure—problematic and partial as it will be—of knowledge of Jews, not "Jews," of some historical possibilities for the ways that Jews have lived their collective lives and imagined them and some future historical possibilities for the continuation of the Jews, not "the Jews" or "the jews," but the Jews. Some of the fury aimed at the initial forays into the world of this thinking (and the fury that might still be coming) may be explicable precisely as the reactions of anti-anti-Semites who hold indeed that the only way to end anti-Semitism is for the Jews effectively to disappear from the earth as a collective, as an entity about which there are some things to be said.

I hope to have furthered the process of thinking about what kind of social identity Jews want to have in the future, an identity not defined by the choice of being a religion among others or a nation requiring as such a state.

My practice here is a kind of radicalism, a neoradicalism, perhaps, that stands in direct opposition to any form of neoliberalism. In this, I have learned much from the black radical traditions: "Black radical praxis aims to dismantle structures of domination that sustain racialized dispossession and exploitation and to imagine and bring into being liberatory possibilities for all oppressed people," critical black studies scholar Charisse Burden-Stelly has written.[8] In the resistance to Sartre, on the part especially of Césaire and Fanon, I have found allies in my own resistance to being disappeared (for my own good, as it were). Nor is this alliance imaginary or only self-serving on my part, for Césaire and Fanon, as well as others in the black radical tradition, have underlined it as well, more than is often remarked.

I deeply associate myself with those who "viewed the solution to the Jewish question in rejecting the division of the globe into distinct units with homogeneous populations rather than establishing precisely such a place for the Jewish people."[9] As we have seen, the latter was considered anti-Zionist and the former defined as Zionism in the first third of the twentieth century. As we have also seen, what was once Zionist, the state of many nations, is now anti-Zionist; what was once anti-Zionist is now Zionism, the nation-state.

I think that halakhic definitions of who is a Jew are appropriate for halakhic purposes, such as weddings, circumcisions, and *aliyot latorah*. And other ways of being Jewish are being found by all sorts of halakhically doubtful Jews. All over Europe and in the United States, too, there are queer (and even not queer) groups devoting themselves to Yiddish culture and the neo-Bund.

No more Federations; Councils; Leadership Committees; sociologists who study Jewish continuity by counting babies and checking out their mothers' "identity."[10] Just Jews, singing, dancing, speaking, and writing in Hebrew, Yiddish, *Judezmo*, learning the Talmud in all sorts of ways, fighting together for justice for Palestinians and Black Lives Matter. I have spent now forty years teaching Talmud to anyone both in the university and in my Sunday morning *shiur*. . . . The embers are there; they don't have to be kindled, but blown on so they burst into flame. I've been trying to write a bellows.

I have emphasized the duality of diaspora as its defining feature in my reimagination of diaspora itself. This duality, however, presages not only a different cultural imagination, one of dual cultural location, but also a different political imagination, one of dual and complex loyalty. Above, I articulated diaspora as a complex cultural situation in which cultural creativity takes place in two spaces, a localized location of culture in which Jews and others participate in the making of culture and a transnational location in which Jews participate with other Jews in other places in the making of Jewish culture in Jewish languages, with Jewish doings, broadly conceived, providing the matrix for such culture making. The same thing applies politically, ethically, and morally.

One way of articulating the broader implications of the ratio of *doikayt* and *Yiddishkayt* is with the halakhic principle that the poor of your own city come before the poor of other cities, an example of the relationship between local economic justice (the poor of one's own place, Jew and non-Jew, to which one has a primary ethical responsibility) and concern for the welfare of Jews everywhere. *Doikayt* signals or indexes another vital moment: stewardship of the land, not the Land of Israel (although that, too), but the planet. As geographer Elissa Sampson once said: "No planet, no Jews!" Note the reversal of the usual construction within which the local is deemed "parochial" and the translocal "universal." A personage known by Jews as Hannagid and in the world as Ibn Nagrela is a perfect figure of diasporic culture understood in this way: Hannagid, in addition to being a great talmudist and Hebrew poet, was appointed vizier in Spain and general of the armies in 1027. As Leon Pinsker wrote of a later time, the mandate then, too, was "to become the sons of their time and their immediate homeland without ceasing to be true Jews."

The No-State Solution

There is a sense in which the very difficulty, the demanding and challenging nature of keeping a culture alive is what produces its value. It has been said: it is the time you wasted on raising the rose that makes it so precious. As anthropologist Henry S. Sharp has written of a First Nations community in Canada: "The old life, even the mid-twentieth-century version of bush life, was taxing. It placed great demands on body and soul. The struggle to survive and achieve some security placed a premium on knowledge, endurance, and constant effort. The harsher conditions were, the more challenging mere survival was, the more bush life engaged the body, mind, and soul of those who lived it and filled them with purpose."[11]

The same is true for the survival of Jewish national life. The greater challenge of living differently from everyone around us, of the commitment involved in learning a language or languages, of studying and understanding a notoriously challenging text, the more the person is filled with purpose. This, then, is what I have been thinking. If we want the Jews to continue as a meaningful entity, a diasporic nation with a culture and the capacity to care deeply and struggle for the oppressed of other nations as well (especially for the nation *we* have oppressed, the Palestinians), we have to make it so: ‏אם תרצו אין זו אגדה‎! If we will it, it is no fairy tale.

Notes

Preface

1. Boyarin, *Judaism*.

2. A "lead" is "any fracture or passageway through ice which is navigable by surface vessels." Government of Canada, *Ice Glossary*, https://www.canada.ca/en/environment-climate-change/services/ice-forecasts-observations/latest-conditions/glossary.html (accessed 16 February 2022). I am grateful to Carlin Barton for this term and reference.

3. For an account of which, see http://jtr.shanti.virginia.edu/volume-1-number-1/gibbs-why-textual-reasoning/.

Introduction

1. The latter is sometimes called "ethnicity" (not that anyone quite knows what that means). See for the nonce Gitelman, *Religion or Ethnicity?* In California today, "ethnicity" seems to be a PC term for "race," since "African American" and something still called, grotesquely, "Caucasian" are options.

2. For extended discussion and complication of this claim, see Anidjar, *Blood*. Anidjar's book has proven a very important conversation partner in my developing thinking for this book.

3. See Anidjar, "Secularism," 67.

4. Epstein, "Social Ontology." See too Hacking, "Making Up People."

5. See Boyarin, *Unheroic Conduct*.

6. For the philosophically inclined, it should be clear that I am not adopting a nominalist position. I believe that there are dogs even if no human is around to perceive them or speak of them but not religions, nations, genders, or money.

7. Sahlins, *Boundaries*.

8. Barton and Boyarin, *Imagine No Religion* and much literature cited there. See especially Asad, *Genealogies of Religion*, chapter 1.

NOTES TO PAGES 5-14

9. Boyarin, *Judaism*.

10. Ritchie, "Neither Fate nor Fiction," 11.

11. I wish to thank here especially my friend Professor Ishay Rosen-Zvi, who pushed me toward stronger (and more honest) attention to some cracks in the foundation here.

12. Collini, "Living in the Love of the Common People," 11.

13. Raz-Krakotzkin, "Exile within Sovereignty: Critique of 'The Negation of Exile' in Israeli Culture," 395–96.

14. Ophir and Rosen-Zvi, *Goy*.

15. Pianko, *Jewish Peoplehood*. The account of the peregrinations of the Second Vatican Council in attempting to figure out what to call the Jews in *Nostrae Aetate* makes for illuminating reading, a kind of précis of my problematic here. See Connelly, *From Enemy to Brother*, 258–60. I am grateful for this reference to Ishay Rosen-Zvi.

16. Ritchie, "Neither Fate nor Fiction," 13–14.

17. Sand, *The Invention of the Jewish People*.

18. Sand, *The Invention*, 21.

19. My century here begins with Leuba, *A Psychological Study of Religion*, 339–63, who famously shows that there are fifty extant definitions of religion that contradict each other as to what is in and what is out. For more recent literature, see the nearly classic by now Asad, *Genealogies of Religion*; Fitzgerald, *The Ideology of Religious Studies*; and Fitzgerald, *Discourse on Civility and Barbarity*. By now, one could say, there is something like a small library of these discussions.

20. Sand, *The Invention*, 21.

21. https://www.tabletmag.com/jewish-arts-and-culture/culture-news/282694/justice-david-wecht-antisemitism.

22. Michaels, "Race into Culture." The next paragraphs on Michaels are adapted from Boyarin and Boyarin, "Diaspora," with the permission of Boyarin.

23. One of his examples is anthropologist Melville Herskovits. Herskovits had argued that African practices were retained by house slaves who had been acculturated into the white culture through a process of "reabsorption" of "Africanisms." To this Michaels reacts, "If you were trained as a house slave, why would absorbing Africanisms count as reabsorbing them?" (Michaels, "Race into Culture," 679). The function of this claim for Herskovits, as Michaels correctly argues, is precisely to avoid the necessity for assuming any "innate endowment" of cultural traits in order to bolster his argument for the African component of African American culture. At this point, however, Michaels jumps to the following: "To make what they did part of your past, there must be some prior assumption of identity between you and them, and this

assumption is as racial to Herskovits as it is in [Countee] Cullen or [Oliver] La Farge. The things the African Negro used to do count as the American Negro's past only because both the African and the American are 'the Negro.' Herskovits's anti-racist culturalism can only be articulated through a commitment to racial identity" ("Race into Culture," 680). Indeed. But this demonstration, repeated over and over in Michaels's essay, does not in any way imply that cultural practices are "innately endowed," as racialist (and racist) theories of cultural differentiation had been wont to argue before the intervention of culturalists such as Franz Boas and his followers, whose work had been largely accomplished by the 1920s.

Let us think for a moment how Herskovits's "house slaves" might have come to feel a sense of identity with the field slaves who had not been acculturated to the white norm. First of all, they might indeed have managed to remember—simply not forget—that their immediate ancestors had been Africans in Africa. Second, their bodies were marked as being different from the other people doing "white" things. Third, they shared a slave status with the field hands. Fourth, the notion of complete separation followed by reestablished contact is a pure fiction. Much more plausible would be a model of acculturation whereby these house slaves had been exposed to the culture of the other slaves that they had partially forgotten during the process of (presumably) early childhood "acculturation" to the house culture and that indeed they might then reabsorb as adults.

24. Michaels, "Race into Culture," 682.

25. Michaels, "Race into Culture," 683.

26. While much of my early argument on Paul in Boyarin, *A Radical Jew* could use nuancing and correction, I stand by this crucial claim.

27. See Kletenick and Neis, "What's the Matter with Jewish Studies?"

28. See Wolfson on Heidegger: *The Duplicity of Philosophy's Shadow*, 53.

29. For a different, but not antithetical, version of this ethical quest, see Mendes-Flohr, *Cultural Disjunctions*. Mendes-Flohr emphasizes more—quite properly, I add—the so-called religious dimensions of *Judaïté* that I, in my search for expansiveness, underemphasize, losing something important therewith. On the other hand, Mendes-Flohr's virtual dismissal of diaspora nationalism and/or Bundism denies a significant dimension of Jewish vitality in the present (rooted in the past) and for the future (*Cultural Disjunctions*, 14).

30. Nussbaum and respondents, *For Love of Country*, 4.

31. Appiah, *Cosmopolitanism*.

32. Appiah, *Cosmopolitanism*, 24.

33. Appiah, *Cosmopolitanism*, 14.

34. Appiah, *Cosmopolitanism*, 50–51.

35. By the way, and relevant at this point, Appiah doesn't quite get Orthodox Judaism at all. There are no rituals for purifying oneself if one has inadvertently eaten nonkosher foods. Indeed, the most plausible response would be guilt and disgust (*pace* Appiah, *Cosmopolitanism*, 52).

36. Appiah, *Cosmopolitanism*, 53.

37. Robbins, "Comparative Cosmopolitanisms," 171.

38. Aimé Césaire, Député for Martinique, to Maurice Thorez, Secretary General of the French Communist Party, October 1956, quoted in Robin D. G. Kelley's introduction to Césaire's *Discourse on Colonialism* ("A Poetics of Anticolonialism," 25–26). I found this quotation, which I adopt as my own, in Okiji, *Jazz as Critique*.

39. Appiah, *Cosmopolitanism*, 80–81.

40. Appiah, *Cosmopolitanism*, 111.

41. Robbins, "Introduction Part I," 2.

42. Clifford, review of *Orientalism*, by Edward W. Said.

43. Clifford, review of *Orientalism*, by Edward W. Said, 222.

44. Breckenridge et al., *Cosmopolitanism*, 5. I totally agree with this statement, despite finding the usage of "derring do" here rather odd.

45. Clifford, review of *Orientalism*, by Edward W. Said, 222. I have proposed earlier a Wittgensteinian "forms of life," which Wittgenstein himself uses as an alternative term for "culture."

46. Robbins, "Comparative Cosmopolitanisms," 173. Pheng Cheah interrogates, "If nationalism as a mode of consciousness and the nation-state as an institution are both undesirable and outmoded, it is not entirely clear what the alternatives are and whether these alternatives actually exist or are capable of being realized" (Cheah, "Introduction Part II," 21). Cheah's tight association of nationalism with the nation-state actually seemingly obscures other possibilities than the cosmopolitan option that he regards as the only even thinkable one.

47. Robbins, "Introduction Part I," 3.

Chapter 1. Just-So Stories

1. For an instructively parallel account of Indian historiography of "triumph," see Pandey, "In Defense of the Fragment."

2. Cooper, *We Keep the Dead Close*.

3. Werbner, "The Place Which Is Diaspora," 29, has produced a brilliant analysis of this "spatial" version of diaspora thinking.

4. Gruen, *Diaspora*.

5. Cf. Levy and Weingrod, *Homelands and Diasporas*, 4, who get this exactly upside down, in my opinion.

6. "However, the term diaspora in the Septuagint translation is not in close co-occurrence with Hebrew galut. Relatively frequent in those passages [where Hebrew has galut] is the Greek word aikhmalosia 'captivity' (from aikhmē 'spear' + (h)alōsis 'taking captive') and its derivations (this is the case in two passages of Daniel, the one of Esdras, and those of Ezekiel, Isaiah, and Abdias 1:11); Daniel 12:7 has dia-skorpismos 'scattering' (a synonym of diaspora, with the same polysemy), Jeremiah has once ptosis 'fall' (29:22); the idea of a change of domicile is expressed by the translators of Jeremiah 52:31 by the Greek verb apoikizesthai, whereas the translators of Abdias (Obadiah) 1:31 used the noun metoikesia, and those of 4 (or 2) Kings 7:35 apoikesia for the same idea." Zgusta, "Diaspora," 292. Gruen, *Diaspora*.

7. *Legat.* 203, 281; *Flacc.* 46. Cf. Strabo 4.1.4; 10.4.17. Thanks to Steve Mason.

8. Boyarin, *A Traveling Homeland*, 33–53.

9. For this as the correct reading here, see Lieberman, *Greek in Jewish Palestine*, 141, and not Ḥanina as in the printed texts. For the topos of Roman clemency toward Jews and Jewish brutality, see Josephus *Wars* I.11.

10. Lieberman, *Greek in Jewish Palestine*, 140.

11. According to the Tosefta (Bab. Qam. 7.3), this was Rabbi Yoḥanan ben Zakkai, centuries earlier than our Rabbi Yoḥanan who made this statement. See discussion by Gafni, "Land, Center and Diaspora Jewish Constructs," 63. Gafni argues that notions like these were confined to the earlier strata of rabbinic literature, "up to and including the Bar-Kochba war (132–135)." For my purpose here, this doesn't matter, since when the Babylonian Talmud quotes the view, it is "canonical" for them, simultaneous with everything else in the text. Nonetheless, from the historical point of view, Gafni's demonstration of a big shift among Palestinian rabbis after the revolt is compelling and important.

12. Rubenstein, "Addressing the Attributes of the Land of Israel," discussed further below.

13. Gafni, "Babylonian Rabbinic Culture," 224. See also the illuminating pages in Gafni on the identification of biblical sites with local late antique Babylonian ones and the cultural role of these identifications (228–30).

14. Dimitrovsky, "Do the Jews Have a Middle Ages?"

15. Boyarin, *A Traveling Homeland*.

16. Raz-Krakotzkin, "Exile within Sovereignty" is one of the richest expressions of such a turn, albeit one that is slightly different in tone from my own. I suspect that it is not a question of right or wrong here, not at all, but the product of some difference of standpoint.

17. Raz-Krakotzkin, "Exile within Sovereignty: Critique of 'The Negation of Exile' in Israeli Culture" and especially the fuller Hebrew version: Raz-Krakotzkin, "Exile within Sovereignty: Toward a Critique of the 'Negation of Exile' in Israeli Culture." Raz-Krakotzkin, "Exile within Sovereignty: Critique of 'The Negation of Exile' in Israeli Culture," 393–94. This entire essay, which is a severely abridged version of the Hebrew version, is crucial.

18. "Unjews": https://www.facebook.com/TabletMag/posts/natan-sharansky-and-gil-troy-we-call-these-critics-un-jews-because-they-believe-/10160571091049691/.

19. For the cutting edge of recent historiography of Zionism, see Pianko, *Zionism and the Roads Not Taken*; Shumsky, *Beyond the Nation-State*.

20. I am aware of the irony that both *Judezmo* and *Judaïté* are derived precisely from European languages themselves but they have been adopted by non-Ashkenazi Jews. *Yiddishkayt* has not.

21. Raz-Krakotzkin, "Exile within Sovereignty: Critique of 'The Negation of Exile' in Israeli Culture," 395–96.

22. Raz-Krakotzkin, "Exile within Sovereignty: Critique of 'The Negation of Exile' in Israeli Culture," 398. Raz-Krakotzkin writes, for instance, "The yearning for redemption is based on the consciousness of exile and as such requires a turn to the oppressed foundations within a culture via undermining the memory of the rulers. It is therefore an action carried out in reality and is based on bestowing value to the viewpoint of the oppressed, a viewpoint *necessary* for a moral position to be developed. Consequently, only defining reality as exile can lead to the moral values that should guide political action." Or again, "Bi-nationalism is a *moral* position that directs the attitude toward reality" (416). Without denying the power and necessity of Raz-Krakotzkin's theological mode of thinking, I find myself thinking much more prosaically, not so much about moral foundations, but about governmental structures that enable and empower rich cultural and social lives for folks of different cultures occupying the same or overlapping spaces and about the natures of those rich and creative collective lives.

23. Boyarin, *A Traveling Homeland*.

Chapter 2. Bad Faith

1. A very fine—in my opinion—attempt to account for this state of affairs by using the notion of the usages of "religion" as bearing a family resemblance to each other has been made by Saler, *Conceptualizing Religion*.

2. For further reading on this topic, see Barton and Boyarin, *Imagine No Religion*, as well as quite a small host by now of other scholars and writers cited here and there.

Specifically with respect to "Judaism," Batnitzky, *How Judaism Became a Religion*; and Boyarin, *Judaism*. For critical commentary on the last-mentioned work, see Barbu, "Discussion of Judaism." This very thoughtful and discerning critical paper finally misses the main point, to wit, what is lost, hidden, occluded when we use second-order terms drawn from our culture that are demonstrably not present in the other that we hope to understand somehow. Perhaps an analogy will help. Let us say that anthropologists wish to describe a culture in which men and women do not pair-bond, generally having widespread and frequent sexual interactions with different members of the group. Sometimes a woman may decide to live with a particular man for a spate of time, but she may—and does—pick up and leave whenever she feels like it. The children of the group belong to their mothers and all the men. Would it make sense to speak of "marriage" among such a group (pretty close to some actually existing human cultures), or should we rather speak of a culture without marriage? Which way do we learn more and occlude less?

3. This and what follows have been drawn (and quartered) from my own recent work arguing these historical points at length: Boyarin, *Judaism*.

4. As Mufti has written with reference to the eighteenth century, "My aim here is to understand the manner in which the Jews of Europe became a *question*, both for themselves and for others, and the implication this being put in question has for elaborating responses . . . to the crises and conflicts of the projects of modernity in European and non-European . . . settings" (*Enlightenment in the Colony*, 10).

5. Mufti, *Enlightenment in the Colony*, 7–8.

6. Let me attempt to be as clear and transparent as I can. I am not vaunting a particular past situation of the Jews as in any sense a panacea for Jewish (or any other) existence in the future as a vital and ethical collective.

7. For a description of the effects of that self-definition in modernity, see Raz-Krakotzkin, "Exile within Sovereignty: Critique of 'The Negation of Exile' in Israeli Culture," 400–401, and for a fuller (Hebrew) version of his argument, Raz-Krakotzkin, "Exile within Sovereignty: Toward a Critique of the 'Negation of Exile' in Israeli Culture."

8. For discussion of this point, see now Whitebook, *Freud*, 377–80, esp. 380.

9. Walzer, "Anti-Zionism and Anti-Semitism."

10. Ernest Renan, "What Is a Nation?" 11. The forgotten things are the discreditable actions of the nation in the past, for example, slavery in the United States. Walzer, "Anti-Zionism and Anti-Semitism," also makes it clear that anti-Zionism is *not* tantamount to anti-Semitism. As he puts it, the problem he has with anti-Zionism is that it is anti-Zionism—and, according to him, wrong—and not that it is covert or

NOTES TO PAGES 38–40

overt anti-Semitism. After all, as recently as one hundred years ago, the vast majority of Jews in the world and an overwhelming majority of Orthodox (and Reform) rabbis were bitterly opposed to Zionism, just about as bitterly as today they might brand anti-Zionism as anti-Semitism. It must be admitted, however, that Walzer somewhat muddies this clarity by insinuating that those who oppose a Jewish state are hypocritical, or at any rate fatally inconsistent in their critiques by incoherently singling out the Jews among all peoples denied a state. This allegation suggests that those folks have a special reason to pick out or pick on the Jews without quite naming that special reason as anti-Semitism.

11. See Anidjar, "Secularism," 59, 62.

12. Anidjar, "Secularism," 74.

13. Mufti, *Enlightenment in the Colony*, 51.

14. See Tzuberi, " 'Reforesting' Jews."

15. Weinreich, *History of the Yiddish Language*, 164.

16. Cited in Batnitzky, *How Judaism Became a Religion*, 3. Shlomo Sand, on the other hand, seems to think that the concept of religion has no history and needs no genealogy, writing, for example, that prior to the putative invention of the "Jewish People," the Jews had been "merely a religious community that lived in the shadow of other, hegemonic religions" (Sand, *The Invention*, 74, 141, and passim). In the second cited passage, Sand refers to the "secularization of the Jewish exile," as if even the critique of the notions of the secular and secularization has never occurred (see Asad, *Formations of the Secular* and a host of others by now). All of Sand's historiographical sophistication with respect to "nation" and "exile" seems to disappear entirely when he speaks of religion: "The devotees of the Old Testament's Judaic faith rejected the salvation of the world that Jesus brought with his sacrifice" (135). Unless Sand is speaking here with heavy irony, this is simply a statement of astonishing naivete. So taken is he with his notion of a "religion" that he even dehistoricizes the concept of "conversion" and hardly even notices that when ancient historians Josephus and Strabo talk about groups being added to the Jewish polity, the terms used are adoption of Jewish laws and acceptance of circumcision and not alleged conversion to a religion. He borders on dishonest when he reads in Josephus *Antiquities* 13.15 (paragraph 397) "because its inhabitants would not bear to change their religious rites for those peculiar to the Jews." Josephus's Greek, of course, reads no such thing: ἐς πάτρια τῶν Ἰουδαίων ἔθη μεταβαλεῖσθαι means "They could not bear to change their customs into the customary ancestral practices of the Judeans."

17. Salaymeh and Lavi, "Religion Is Secularized Tradition." I wish to thank the authors of this essay for providing me access prior to its publication and also for the

work's bibliographical references and discussions, which have helped me tremendously in working out the argument of this chapter. For a concise and helpful account of "Judaism" becoming a "religion" in the early modern period, see Batnitzky, *How Judaism Became a Religion;* and Stern, *Jewish Materialism*, 9–10.

18. Salaymeh and Lavi, "Religion Is Secularized Tradition." Even more sharply, they state their objective—which matches mine—"to refine the existing legal-analytical tools for evaluating *how* states discriminate against religious minorities under the doctrine of religious freedom."

19. Salaymeh and Lavi, "Religion Is Secularized Tradition." It should be pointed out for record that the authors of the essay are careful not to essentialize Protestantism or to assign it as the only cause for the developments; I would suggest that Protestant thought is the enabling condition, rather than cause, of the process of secular production of "religion." See the very important essay by Samuel Moyn, which nuances and complexifies these formulae without, I think, discrediting them ("From Communist to Muslim").

20. Opines the court: "The circumcision changes the child's body permanently and irreparably. This change runs contrary to the interests of the child in deciding his religious affiliation later in life" (Aumüller, "Unofficial Translation"). This is factually erroneous, owing to the empirical fact that over the centuries, quite large numbers of Jews circumcised on the eighth day have chosen Christianity without let or hindrance. One could, in fact, argue that the sort of religious indoctrination certainly allowed by the Cologne court is a more powerful hindrance to the free choice of religion than circumcision.

21. Salaymeh and Lavi, "Religion Is Secularized Tradition." See the claim made by Saba Mahmood (זכרה ברוך) and Peter Danchin, who argue that "in all modern states we can see a consistent pattern of protecting state-sanctioned traditions or dominant religions and a corresponding insensitivity to and denial of the claims of minority, nontraditional, or unpopular religious groups" ("Immunity or Regulation?" 154).

22. Of course, at the same time, I would defend the "right" of grown individuals to choose to respond to that thrownness in their own fashion, including the right to convert to Christianity, despite their (when male) circumcised state and even the lack of recognition of such conversion from the (theoretical) Jewish perspective. Interestingly, this seems to be the correct interpretation of *German* law itself, notwithstanding the perverse reasoning of the Cologne court (Fateh-Maghadam, "Criminalizing Male Circumcision?").

23. Cf. Dirks, "The Policing of Tradition."

24. Kant, "Religion within the Bounds of Bare Reason," 69. Kant, of course, operates under the modern and European notion that "political laws" and a church are mutually exclusive entities, the opposition rejected here, a necessary rejection for the further delineation of the Jews as a nation.

25. Boyarin, "Anna O(Rthodox)."

26. Gitelman, *Religion or Ethnicity?* For more extended discussion of this issue than I can provide here, see Boyarin, *Judaism.*

27. Lyall, "British High Court Says School's Ethnic-Based Admissions Policy Is Illegal."

28. Lyall, "British High Court Says School's Ethnic-Based Admissions Policy Is Illegal."

29. Rosenzweig, *The Star of Redemption*, 342. Professor Manuel d'Olivera, from whom I learned of this quotation, misreads it, I think, when he writes: "There is but a small step between the identification of oneself as the contents of one's belief and the integration of the divine nature intrinsic to that contents that initiates the process of 'self-deification.' " But more on this anon.

30. In support of this reading, see Haggai Dagan, who writes, "Rosenzweig does not attempt to conceal this aspect of his thought in his book: 'It [the people of Israel] does not have to hire the services of the spirit; the natural propagation of the body guarantees it eternity.' All this is stated explicitly: The Jewish people does not rely upon the spirit, or upon its intellectual or ethical uniqueness, or upon one or another mental quality, or even upon tradition or culture, but only upon blood ties and natural procreation" ("Motif of Blood," 244). This is somehow structurally similar to the conclusion of another existentialist that Jews would not exist at all were it not for the hostility of others—anti-Semitism, in short (Sartre, *Anti-Semite and Jew*). And yet somehow it carries the opposite effect and affect.

31. Williams, "To the North," 8.

32. Boyarin and Boyarin, "Diaspora."

Chapter 3. Bad Blood

1. Gil Anidjar has tied the blood symbol at its point of origin to war: "War was a consequence of blood and its logical end. It was conducted for blood motives (family and tribe, lust and revenge). It maintained and reproduced itself as the culmination of innumerable and massive instances of blood feuds" (Anidjar, *Blood*, 3).

2. Anidjar, *Blood*, 7.

3. Anidjar, *Blood*, 25–26.

4. Anidjar, "We Have Never Been Jewish," 37.

NOTES TO PAGES 51-55

5. Rosenzweig, *The Star of Redemption*, 298.

6. Anidjar, *Blood*, 44–49.

7. Appiah, *The Ethics of Identity*, 237.

8. Boyarin and Boyarin, "Diaspora."

9. Anderson, *Imagined Communities*, 11. He, moreover, draws clear distinctions between the nation and the nation-state, writing, "If nation-states are widely conceded to be 'new' and 'historical,' the nations to which they give political expression always loom out of an immemorial past, and, still more important, glide into a limitless future. It is the magic of nationalism to turn chance into destiny." On this distinction I will have much to say in other parts of my manifesto.

10. Sartre, *Anti-Semite and Jew*, 64, as cited in Lapidot, *Jews out of the Question*, 76.

11. Sartre, *Anti-Semite and Jew*, 98–99.

12. Dagan, "Blood and Myth," 153.

13. Dagan, "Blood and Myth," 153.

14. Ho, *The Graves of Tarim*, xxii.

15. See, however, Wolfson's arguably more sensitive and nuanced account of Rosenzweig (*The Duplicity of Philosophy's Shadow*, 71–73). I believe that our two readings are compatible and surely converge in our judgment that Rosenzweig is not making a racist argument or claim.

16. Boyarin and Boyarin, "Diaspora."

17. Dagan, "Blood and Myth," 153. On the other hand, I would contest Dagan's declaration: "One should therefore ask what kind of a mental atmosphere his views create. I would argue that they create an atmosphere in which this technical-restricting definition of identity, constituted by relation to the mother, becomes a substantive characterization of Judaism on a biological basis: blood and birth" (153). I would argue, in turn, that Rosenzweig here does not create an atmosphere; he describes it sharply and accurately, providing also the cure for its obvious risks of racialism or even racism, precisely in that insistence (cited above in my text) that there is absolutely no essence whatever implied by that nexus of blood and birth. It is here that I part company with Dagan almost completely, as he denies the historical reality, not only of the actual "blood ties" of the Jews to each other, but even of the representation of such ties as a Rosenzweig-invented myth (154). I agree to the first proposition, but not the second, not at all. The representation of the Children of Israel as an ethnic group joined by genealogy goes back at least to the Bible; that is what Rosenzweig refracts and reflects. To be sure, any such racialized myth would have to be modern, but Dagan himself has shown us the way to a nonracialized reading of Rosenzweig!

18. Dagan, "Motif of Blood," 242.

19. Dagan, "Blood and Myth," 153.

20. Rabinow, "Representations Are Social Facts."

21. I want to acknowledge here Dr. El'ad Lapidot, who has been singularly helpful to me in thinking through these claims as well as much else.

22. Butler, "Performative Agency."

23. Butler, "Performative Agency," 149.

24. See Fred Moten: "The new speech, which animates Césaire's poetry as well as Fanon's invocation of Césaire in the interest of disavowing the new speech, is where we discover, again and again, the various and unrecoverable natality that we share" (*The Universal Machine*, 216).

25. In a sense, then, the convert (or rather the act of conversion) is the "ideal type"—in the Weberian sense—of *Judaïté*, because, and only because, it manifests the performativity of Jewish identity explicitly and openly, even celebratorily. The right practices are practiced and the right words said by the right person and the person becomes a Jew by *fiat accompli*, by birth and blood, as all us Jews are.

Chapter 4. *Judaïtude*/Négritude

1. Césaire called the movement Négritude in his famous *Discourse on Colonialism*. Rabaka, *The Negritude Movement*, provides a good introduction to his movement.

2. Saussy, *Are We Comparing Yet?* 93–95. For this reading, see also Bernasconi, "The European Knows and Does Not Know," 105: "Furthermore, although Sartre identified Negritude as 'an anti-racist racism,' a phrase that Fanon later employed for himself, . . . by declaring that Negritude gives way to the idea of the proletariat, Sartre located Negritude as a stage in the dialectic and thereby robbed Fanon of his Negritude." Note that one does not have to claim that Fanon was not critical of Césaire's (or Senghor's) Négritude—nor is it possible—in order for him to be shocked and dismayed on discovering that Sartre intended his racial difference with all it entailed to be simply sublated. Bernasconi writes, and I concur, "Fanon is widely identified as a critic of the negritude movement. This impression is at best the result of an oversimplification of his rich and complex argument" ("The Assumption of Negritude," 76).

3. Saussy, *Are We Comparing Yet?* 101.

4. Sartre, *Black Orpheus*, 59–60.

5. Fanon, *Black Skin, White Masks*, 112.

6. It is, of course, well known by now that in Fanon's later writings, "we see him firing red-hot broadsides into Negritude, and condemning it in the most radical terms throughout his work" (Memmi, "The Impossible Life of Frantz Fanon," 17).

Memmi gives an astute account of Fanon's turn to "universalism" toward the end of his life (29).

7. Cf., for quite a different take on this passage in Fanon, Rabaka, *Forms of Fanonism*, 71–72. I am, as I've said in the text, quite close in my reading of Fanon with Saussy's. It was indeed Saussy's work that reminded me of this passage in Fanon and sent me to reread the work after some thirty years: " 'When I read this page,' said Fanon in 1952, 'I sensed that my last chance was being taken away from me.' A little sacrifice is demanded for the sake of the world proletariat—very little, in the larger order of things—just an erasure of your markedness, which as we know is in the nature of a supplement to that regular order of things. But there is a 'larger' or 'regular' order of things only from a certain perspective, and Fanon will not go along with it. 'I am not a possibility of something else, I am fully what I am. It is not incumbent on me to pursue the universal.' " Saussy, *Are We Comparing Yet?* 101.

See too Boyarin and Boyarin, "Diaspora," on Lyotard, esp. 699–701 on Lyotard's sublation of the Jews into the jews. I am not asserting here that Fanon was a proponent of Senghor's or Césaire's version of Négritude. The good faith of my approach to Césaire and Fanon in a polemic essentially about Jews has been called into question. Just for the record, it seems to me that it needs no defense or justification, given the analogies (not quite homologies) that those two authors expressed passionately between Jews and blacks, most movingly perhaps in Césaire's powerful "When I switch on my radio and hear that black men are being lynched in America, I say that they have lied to us: Hitler isn't dead. When I switch on my radio and hear that Jews are being insulted, persecuted, and massacred, I say that they have lied to us: Hitler isn't dead" (cited from memory in Fanon, *Black Skin, White Masks*, 70). See too, for a quite different reading of Fanon's encounter with Sartre, Memmi, "The Impossible Life," 18–19.

8. I thus reject Memmi's reading of Fanon as having abandoned his Négritude:

He could have concluded by identifying with his misfortune and trying to confront it directly in order to transform it. Or he could have evaded it, an alternative reaction common to many oppressed; and in the end that is what he chose to do. This choice had decisive consequences for his subsequent work. The first of these was his totally negative and very questionable conception of Negritude. After all, Negritude implies more than the mere consciousness of misfortune and of belonging to a vanquished group. It is also recognition and affirmation of self; it is protest, reconstruction of a culture, at least of its potential, positive adherence to a group, and the decision to contribute to a collective future. The

disdainful abandonment of Blackness (or Jewishness, or Arabness) in the name
of universalism and universal man rests on a misconception. This is not the
place to go into a thorough critique. It should however be pointed out that such
an outlook of false universalism and abstract humanism is based on neglecting
all specific identity and all intervening social particularities, though it is hard to
see why these are necessarily contemptible, nor how they could be dispensed
with. Universal man and universal culture are after all made up of particular
men and particular cultures. (Memmi, "The Impossible Life," 34)

I agree with Memmi's own critique here of "cosmopolitanism," but think he has
missed the conflict, the ambivalence in Fanon himself for which I try here to make a
case. See too Bernasconi, "Assumption of Negritude," 73–74, for Fanon's rejection of
an abstract universalism.

    9. Appiah, foreword, viii.

    10. Fanon, *Black Skin, White Masks*, xii; Bernasconi, "The European Knows and
Does Not Know," 108.

    11. Fanon, *Black Skin, White Masks*, xviii. This "black hole" remains a haunting pres-
ence throughout the book: "After having driven himself to the limits of self-destruction,
the black man, meticulously or impetuously, will jump into the 'black hole' from which
will gush forth 'the great black scream with such force that it will shake the foundations
of the world' " (Fanon, *Black Skin, White Masks*, 175). Bernasconi has written, "However, the fact that Fanon dismisses that conception of negritude that privileged the past
should not lead one to assume that he rejected all conceptions of negritude. It was clear
to Fanon that the negritude movement was not homogeneous and that Senghor and
Césaire represented different conceptions of its potential. And the fact that Fanon uses
the phrase 'Tower of the Past' to characterize what he rejects suggests that he might be
exempting Césaire, who had written, as Fanon repeatedly reminds us, 'My negritude is
neither a tower nor a cathedral' " ("Assumption of Negritude," 73).

    12. Fanon, *Black Skin, White Masks*, 1.

    13. Fanon, *Black Skin, White Masks*, 101.

    14. Fanon, *Black Skin, White Masks*, 106.

    15. Fanon, *Black Skin, White Masks*, 108.

    16. Fanon, *Black Skin, White Masks*, 109–10, citing Césaire.

    17. Fanon, *Black Skin, White Masks*, 111.

    18. Sartre—here, the very fount of existentialism—robs Fanon of his existence by
ascribing an essence to the "Negro" that precedes their existence! (Fanon, *Black Skin,
White Masks*, 114–15).

19. Fanon, *Black Skin, White Masks*, 116–17.

20. Fanon, *Black Skin, White Masks*, 119. Again Bernasconi, "The European Knows and Does Not Know," esp. 106, must be consulted for a deeper, more complex reading that does not, I reckon, contradict or supplant what I offer here.

21. Rabaka, *Forms of Fanonism*, 79.

22. Lapidot, *Jews out of the Question*, 85–148.

23. Lapidot, *Jews out of the Question*, 74.

24. Lapidot, *Jews out of the Question*, 74.

25. Lapidot, *Jews out of the Question*, 74–75.

26. Lapidot, *Jews out of the Question*, 75. Sartre's own posture would have been much richer, I dare say, had he been willing to afford to the Jews the same kinds of historical consciousness as other folks and not based himself on the Zionist reading of the Jewish Diaspora as having stepped out of history entirely. A version of this ambivalence explains, perhaps, also Sartre's ambivalence toward Négritude and that of Césaire and Fanon toward Sartre. This acknowledgment of limitations without rejecting them is, I think, one key to Fanon's evident ambivalence. As Robert Bernasconi has perspicaciously written, "He does not present an external critique of Négritude, but an attempt to engage with it from the inside. However, he does not seem to offer any kind of resolution of the difficulties there. At one point Fanon announces that 'every hand I played was a losing hand.' The final sentence of the chapter reads: 'Irresponsible, straddling Nothingness and Infinity, I began to weep.' He repeatedly describes his experience as that of being in an infernal circle, and in the Introduction he declares the elimination of the vicious circle as the only guideline for his efforts. The question is whether Fanon finds a way out of the vicious circle and, if so, where Césaire stands in relation to that exit" ("Assumption of Negritude," 70).

27. When speaking of the "black man," Fanon has no difficulty at all in referring to the experience of Jews—not that he identifies them, nor do I—but the power of extimacy is palpable.

28. "All they ask of the [black man] is to be a good black; the rest will follow on its own. Making him speak pidgin is tying him to an image, snaring him, imprisoning him as the eternal victim of his own essence, of a *visible appearance* for which he is not responsible. And, of course, just as the Jew who is lavish with his money is suspect, so the black man who quotes Montesquieu must be watched" (Fanon, *Black Skin, White Masks*, 18). Fanon clearly gets it too that the privilege afforded to Jews in our societies is a kind of trap as well: "The Arab is told: 'If you are poor it's because the Jew has cheated you and robbed you of everything.' The Jew is told: 'You're not of the same caliber as the Arab because in fact you are white and you have Bergson and Einstein.'

The black man is told: You are the finest soldiers in the French empire" (Fanon, *Black Skin, White Masks*, 83).

29. Fanon, *Black Skin, White Masks*, 69. Fanon follows this clarion with invocations of Césaire's solidarity with Jews as well. Jonathan Boyarin and I are preparing now a study of Césaire and the Jewish Question.

30. Fanon, *Black Skin, White Masks*, 95.

31. Fanon, *Black Skin, White Masks*, 150. I quite disagree with Bernasconi's reading of this passage ("Assumption of Negritude," 76), as it totally elides (literally under elliptical dots) the contrast with Jews in which the statement functions.

32. That the diaspora nation offers much greater possibilities for a better future for Jews and others is quite a different claim than to propose, *Fiddler on the Roof* style, that everything was all right with Jewish collective life until modern nationalism came along and spoiled it, a claim that would be dishonest and, indeed, ridiculous. The argument is not that we used to do better, but rather about what is the path to do better in the future.

33. For a remarkably concise and lucid explication of this point, see Peter Beinart at https://jewishcurrents.org/there-is-no-right-to-a-state/?fbclid=IwAR1i1sMtz-JH6ZWCte6YGuYe_Nmjn4mI_AcndhcoMioSDeF8okENHWcQ7bc.

34. Haun Saussy reminds me: "This older use of 'nation' can also be found in, e.g., the Collège des Quatre Nations (a subpart of the old Sorbonne formerly housed in the buildings now occupied by the French Academy)" (personal communication, 2021).

35. Hobsbawm, *Nations and Nationalism*, 15–16.

36. Ato Quayson has pointed to the irony of the fact that in the same year that *nación* becomes recognized as a sovereign political entity in the Spanish lexicon, at the Berlin Conference, the Europeans and Americans met as nation-states themselves to divide Africa up into nation-states of its own. At least some of the problems of modern Africa seem to me (and I am no Africanist) to stem from such artificial divisions (personal communication, 2021).

37. Hobsbawm, *Nations and Nationalism*, 17.

38. Hobsbawm, *Nations and Nationalism*, 17–18. Hobsbawm cites as well the *Oxford English Dictionary*, which remarks explicitly that the notion of "political unity and independence" for the *nation* is a recent one—in 1908!

39. The significance of this cannot be more strongly articulated than Aamir Mufti's formulation: "The inherent failure of the modern nation-state system, the recurring crises it engenders about 'national' peoples and 'minorities,' is condensed in concentrated form, and revealed with unrelenting clarity, in the conflict over Pales-

tine and the nature of the Jews and the Palestinians as distinct peoples" (*Enlightenment in the Colony*, 38).

40. Chatterjee, *The Nation*, 3.

41. The transitions in Indian nationalism as described by Chatterjee and those within Jewish nationalism to be detailed below are, it seems to me, strikingly parallel. (Nor is this accident—entirely. See the illuminating summary discussion of Mufti, *Enlightenment in the Colony*, 2–14, as well as the development of these ideas throughout his enlightening book, and 19–20 "on the crisis of authenticity" haunting Urdu culture, a discussion that I found curiously comforting in its similarity to the situation of the Jews.) I am reducing a complex and historically detailed argument to its bare bones here, but while Indian nationalism focused initially on the apparently cultural aspects of the nation—languages, literatures, practices—and moved to a primarily political movement at a later stage, a revisionist reading of Jewish nationalism carried out below will reveal comparable stages of development. On India, see Chatterjee, *The Nation*, 28–29 and passim. Especially in his detailed account of Bengali history writing, Chatterjee notes that it was only in the last quarter of the nineteenth century that "the identification in European historiography between the notions of country or people, sovereignty, and statehood is now lodged firmly in the mind of the English-educated Bengali" (95). For Jews educated in German historiographical traditions, in which *Deutschtum* was not lodged in a single state by any means—and still isn't—this identification may have been slower to arrive.

42. Moten, *The Universal Machine*; Moten, *Stolen Life*; Moten, *Black and Blur*. The overall title of Moten's trilogy is *Consent Not to Be a Single Being* (taken from Édouard Glissant).

43. Abandoning thus any dualistic accounts of these domains as hierarchically distinguished, as "inner" and "outer" or "material" and "spiritual" in Platonic-Christian mode, let's consider them as spatially distinct, one facing inward and one facing outward but on the same level of materiality. There will be no more distinction—as there never was before, in any case—between cultural and political. Where Chatterjee seems to be reading the "spiritual" as indeed spiritual, a realm of inner contemplation and self-knowledge (*The Nation*, 48–49), I am going to shift it into the realm of the form of life of the nation. While for Chatterjee, the "material" is indeed material, the realm of making and doing and manipulation of objects, I am going to take it as the spaces of shared, *necessarily* shared practice (such as maintaining the roads and the hospitals), those overlaps of identification that enable a polity of more than one nation to coexist. See the riveting discussion in Stern, *Jewish Materialism*, 18–20, on the entailments of materialism in the making of nations. Neither space is more material

or more spiritual than the other; neither is private versus public; neither is secular versus "religious," and neither is entirely cut off from the other, or even cut off at all.

44. Shumsky, *Beyond the Nation-State.*

Chapter 5. Zionism without Israel

1. For recent historiography, see Pianko, *Zionism and the Roads Not Taken*; Shumsky, *Beyond the Nation-State.*

2. Chatterjee, *The Nation*, 11.

3. Shumsky, *Beyond the Nation-State. Gaeltacht* (pl. Gaeltachtaí) is an Irish term referring individually to any, or collectively to all, of the districts where the government recognizes that the Irish language is the predominant vernacular, or language of the home. Of course, the imagined space of Jewish autonomy in Palestine as conceived by early Zionism would be much more than a space for cultivation or preservation of a language.

4. This fits perfectly not only with Chatterjee's image of the political nationalism of the ex-colony being forced to fit into the forms of Western European nationalism but also with Homi Bhabha's descriptions of the ambivalent (to Bhabha too) mimic-men of colonialism. See "Of Mimicry and Men." Herzl is, it seems, according to that regnant interpretation, exemplary of the turn to nationalism as ethnic politics that Chatterjee remarks as the particular later form that nationalism takes.

5. Shumsky, *Beyond the Nation-State*, 45.

6. Shumsky, *Beyond the Nation-State*, 79.

7. Shumsky, *Beyond the Nation-State*, 50, 89. See too Bhabha, "Of Mimicry and Men."

8. Shumsky, *Beyond the Nation-State*, 59.

9. Bhabha, "Of Mimicry and Men."

10. Boyarin, "The Colonial Drag."

11. Shumsky, *Beyond the Nation-State*, 84.

12. Fanon, *Black Skin, White Masks*, 2–3.

13. It is striking how Fanon describes the relation of the black bourgeoisie in Martinique to Creole. The vicious response of such as Herzl to Yiddish is so close as to be nearly palpable.

14. *Pace* an anonymous sniper, this claim has nothing to do with me being an "Orthodox Jew," any more than Fanon is writing from the point of view of an African religionist.

15. See discussion of this thinking in Shumsky, *Beyond the Nation-State*, 57–59, for further elaboration and explanation of this seeming paradox in Herzl's thought.

Shumsky fascinatingly shows that bilingualism, that is, the language of a specific nation alongside German, was considered an integral part of the national culture by nationalist thinkers. I have encountered this phenomenon myself. Some twenty years ago, an Egyptian professor in her sixties was quite shocked to find out that we don't all speak French fluently: "But you are Jews, aren't you?" she asked incredulously. North African Jews speaking French was marked for this person as a typically Jewish cultural performance, supporting via parallel Shumsky's interpretation of Herzl's claim for German. Among the examples offered by Shumsky are Czech and Slovenian. In some cases, the national language was afforded primacy, with German bearing a secondary role; in some cases the opposite. Shumsky compares Herzl's attitude toward German culture for the Jews to that second option, with Yiddish as the secondary language. Where Shumsky's argument on this point breaks down quite completely, in my opinion, is when he goes on to compare an important Sephardic Zionist thinker of the same time as Herzl himself, the Tunisian historian and journalist Nissim Malul (1892–1959). In Shumsky's view, Malul espoused "cultural-national approaches clearly paralleled [to those of] Herzl and Nordau" (75). They are parallel, according to Shumsky, because Malul manifested deep attachment to Arabic and Arabic culture as well as passionate concern for Jewish national culture in Hebrew. The positions, however, could not be further apart. Herzl demands that the primary national cultural language be the language of a land and an empire far away (with appropriate refresher trips every couple of years), a language that would separate the Jews in Palestine from their non-Jewish neighbors as well as from the entire circumambient world, while Malul argues for development of a bilingual culture in which Jews participated in the local language world of Palestine and the surrounding Arabic people as well as developing their Hebrew, national culture. Malul would be similar to Herzl had he proposed that the Jews of Palestine speak *French* and Hebrew—but he didn't.

16. Shumsky, *Beyond the Nation-State*, 91–92.

17. Shumsky, *Beyond the Nation-State*, 100.

18. Shumsky, *Beyond the Nation-State*, 105.

19. I don't say "Israeli," since many Jewish historians who live outside of Israel adopted it as well, and, as demonstrated throughout this manifesto, many Israeli historians have rejected it.

20. Shumsky, *Beyond the Nation-State*, 113.

21. Shumsky, *Beyond the Nation-State*, 47.

22. Shumsky, *Beyond the Nation-State*, 47.

23. Shumsky, *Beyond the Nation-State*, 32–33. I have slightly modified the last sentence, removing a bracketed "the sons of" before "their homeland," because this gloss

is not necessary and weakens the sentence; the meaning is clear that "sons of" governs both "their own time" and "their homeland."

24. Shumsky, *Beyond the Nation-State*, 34.

25. Boyarin, *A Traveling Homeland*.

26. Shumsky, *Beyond the Nation-State*, 36.

Chapter 6. Diaspora Nation

1. Ho, *The Graves of Tarim*, 4n1. He remarks earlier work of "the Boyarins" and others that had already begun to disperse these associations, for example, Boyarin, *A Traveling Homeland* and earlier Boyarin and Boyarin, "Diaspora."

2. A perfect representation of this view that diaspora is a pathology whose only cure is a nation-state, a view that this book sets out to contest, can be found in the long citation by Shlomo Sand of the words of the first historian of the Jews appointed to a chair at the nascent Hebrew University, Itzhak Baer (*The Invention*, 101–2). For Baer, every nation has its natural place on earth—"God gave to every nation its place, and to the Jews he gave Palestine." A nation not occupying that "natural" space is then "unnatural." Regarding "negation of the diaspora," Ho remarks, "Recidivist long-distance nationalisms may travel far, but they hardly expand the time and space of social life. In the global village, they narrow rather than expand the space for internal debate. In old diasporas, in contrast, the space for internal debate is often a large one" (*The Graves of Tarim*, 5).

3. Anzi, "Yemenite Jews in the Red Sea Trade," 71.

4. This is a point again that Sand seems not to get. He is seemingly shocked and delighted that the dean of Israeli Zionist historians, B. Z. Dinur, wrote that "the Russian conquests did not destroy the Khazar kingdom entirely, but they broke it up and diminished it. And this kingdom, which had absorbed Jewish immigrants and refugees from many exiles, must itself have become a diaspora mother, the mother of one of the greatest of the diasporas—of Israel in Russia, Lithuania and Poland" (Dinur, *Israel and the Diaspora*). I can't see for the life of me why a reader today "might be astonished to hear that 'the high priest of memory in the 1950's' described Khazaria as the 'diaspora mother' of Eastern European Jewry" (ibid.). This is no more astonishing than someone describing Iberia as the diaspora mother of Sephardic Jewry.

5. Benor makes clear the exceptional character of Yiddish and *Judezmo* together vis-à-vis all the others in that these two continue(d) to be spoken by Jews in areas where the local languages were of an entirely different character than the Jewish ones (Benor, "Do American Jews?" 236). This has a great deal of significance. It is interest-

ing that both languages are named with a word that means effectively "Jewishness" or "Jewhood." On this general issue, see Benor, "Towards a New Understanding of Jewish Language," 1069.

6. For this elegant formulation in a different context, see Mufti, *Enlightenment in the Colony*, 40. The same tensions have obtained for the conflict between a black radical tradition fighting against economic and other forms of oppression for blacks and for all in the United States and the "culturalism" tendency that seeks (or sought) only a place for blacks and black culture within the American bourgeoisie, as analyzed lucidly by Charisse Burden-Stelly, "Cold War Culturalism and African Diaspora Theory."

7. Some of the material in the next few paragraphs is being recycled from Boyarin, *A Traveling Homeland*.

8. Baumann, "Diaspora," 322.

9. Du Bois, *The World and Africa*, 7.

10. Cohen, *Global Diasporas*, 35.

11. Too many American Jews fall into the category of those "proud ethnics" who "take pleasure in a subjective feeling of ethnic identity, but shy away from the more substantive ethnicity that demands involvement in a concrete community with organizations, mutual commitments, and some elements of constraint" (Hollinger, *Postethnic*, 40).

12. Flood, *Objects of Translation*, 1.

13. Anderson, *Imagined Communities*.

14. Drory, *Models and Contacts*, 184, citing the tenth-century Egyptian Rabbi Sa'adya Gaon for the usage.

15. See here Baron, *Christian Era*, 104.

16. Sand, *The Invention*, 144.

17. Ho, *The Graves of Tarim*, 14.

18. Ho makes this point by showing that within the Muslim community there are "fundamentalists" who destroy the revered graves of Hadrami Sufi saints, but what constitutes them as a "society"—I'm not entirely satisfied with that term—is that there is a set of questions, and "the answers that people develop for these questions stand within one discursive tradition in the sense that they draw on the same texts, authorities, and assumptions to a degree that is seldom acknowledged" (*The Graves of Tarim*, 11). After all, only a Jew can define her- or himself as one who does *not* keep the Shabbos.

19. Cf. Mendes-Flohr, *Cultural Disjunctions*, 42.

20. Appiah, *The Ethics of Identity*, 237.

21. Note how this perspective tends to reduce the "paradoxical predicament" of the Jews in modernity when they are vilified both as particularists who undermine universalist claims and at the same time as "figures of deracination, abstraction," and rootlessness (Mufti, *Enlightenment in the Colony*, 38). Reduce, but not resolve, since the loyalties are, indeed, divided and in tension nonetheless.

22. See too Hollinger, *Postethnic*, 4–5.

23. Arendt, *The Jew as Pariah*, 67. See Mufti, *Enlightenment in the Colony*, 19. We may be able to develop sufficient moral capacity to grieve all lives (see Butler, *Frames of War*), but it is impossible—for me, at any rate—to imagine a universal grieving for all cultural losses without particular communities to grieve them. As we are taught in the present moment (June 10, 2020), "Black Lives Matter" doesn't *only* mean black bodies, but all the makings and doings of black people.

24. Ho, *The Graves of Tarim*, xix.

25. Boyarin and Boyarin, *Powers of Diaspora*.

26. Bevir, "On Tradition," 37.

27. Bevir, "On Tradition," 16. This is not an empirical claim but "a philosophical deduction from the grammar of our concepts."

28. Bevir, "On Tradition," 37.

29. Yadgar, "Tradition," 458.

30. Pearce and Wunsch, *Documents of Judean Exiles*.

31. For full elaboration of these points, see Boyarin, *A Traveling Homeland*.

32. Dimitrovsky, "Do the Jews Have a Middle Ages?"

33. For further reading on this as a historical process, Fishman, *Becoming the People of the Talmud* is essential.

34. Dolgopolski, *What Is Talmud?*

35. See, on the deep meaning of these patterns, Dolgopolski, *What Is Talmud?*

36. Jonathan Boyarin, "Voices around the Text." And see too his recent *Yeshiva Days* for full, rich evocations of one version of these living practices. Finkin, *A Rhetorical Conversation*.

37. See Dolgopolski, *What Is Talmud?*

38. Mendes-Flohr, *Cultural Disjunctions*, 8. See too Shumsky, *Between Prague and Jerusalem* for more of the political entailments of especially Buber's views.

39. The richness of this way of the Talmud is best experienced, for those who are not in it, in some of the great works of Yiddish literature, from the very well-known Shalom Aleikhem to the perhaps less known Chaim Grade.

40. Dimitrovsky, "Do the Jews Have a Middle Ages?"; Fishman, *Becoming the People of the Talmud*; Wimpfheimer, *The "Talmud."*

Chapter 7. The Lullaby of Jewland

1. In my previous discussion of this text (*Traveling Homeland*), I go into more detail on the historical background of the relations between the Babylonian academies and the later foundations in the West. I also go into much more detail on the gendered aspects of the plot. Here I reproduce only what is necessary for the present case.

2. In the early modern period, Yemenite Jews *and Muslims* have played similar roles in their diasporic homes in Ethiopia and Egypt (Anzi, "Yemenite Jews," 91). See especially there: "This shows that not only did Yemenite Jews serve in rabbinical positions and provide religious services, but they were actually involved in the re-creation of rabbinical communities in Ethiopia and India. In this respect, Yemenite Jews served as a bridge between rabbinic European Jews and the Jews of Northeast Africa. This clearly indicates that Yemenite Jews played an important role in creating ties and forging a common identity among Jews in the Red Sea area."

3. Conway, "Spiritual Humor."

4. See the beautiful essay of my teacher, Professor Hayyim Zalman Dimitrovsky, may the memory of the righteous be for a blessing, Dimitrovsky, "Do the Jews Have a Middle Ages?"

5. Moten, *The Universal Machine*, 212.

6. Moten, *The Universal Machine*, 112.

7. See also the crucial Okiji, *Jazz as Critique*.

8. Now, having read Frank Wilderson, I better understand why. See *Afropessimism*.

9. The quotation is from Du Bois, *Black Reconstruction in America*.

10. Moten, *The Universal Machine*, 212–13. Both jargon and pidgin were deemed to have no grammar!

11. Moten, *The Universal Machine*, 224–25.

12. *Mauschel* is the German Jewish one and *Moishele* is the Eastern European one. On *Hochdeutsch*, see also Wolfson, *The Duplicity of Philosophy's Shadow*, 38.

13. Gilman, *Jewish Self-Hatred*; Moten, *The Universal Machine*, 214.

14. Moten, *The Universal Machine*, 215.

15. Moten, *The Universal Machine*, 220.

16. See below for further discussion of this important concept.

17. Wimpfheimer, *The "Talmud."*

18. What, then, can we say about the *sensorium* of the Jews? Cf. Ho, *The Graves of Tarim*, 10n5.

19. Newman, "The Jewish Sound of Speech."

20. For the particular linguistic significance of Talmud-language in Yiddish, see Finkin, *A Rhetorical Conversation*. See too the following: "Jewish languages are often strongly influenced by a language spoken by the group's ancestors. In the case of Yiddish, the main previous Jewish language was Judeo-French. In the case of Judeo-Spanish, the main previous Jewish language was Judeo-Arabic. And in the case of Jewish English, the main previous Jewish language was Yiddish. These previous languages provide influences in lexicon, as well as other areas. In addition, the previous languages have a major impact on the use of Hebrew and Aramaic: which words are used, how they are pronounced, and how they are integrated morpho-syntactically" (Spolsky and Benor, "Jewish Languages," 120). The significant point for my discussion here is that that Hebrew-Aramaic component shared and inherited is the language of the Talmud and liturgy.

21. "The early twentieth century saw a flowering of American Hebrew belles lettres, but it was mostly a continuation of Eastern European Hebraism. The existence of the State of Israel has changed the meaning of Hebrew writing in the Diaspora. Now writing in Hebrew is seen as an act of cultural connection to contemporary Israel, rather than connection to local, international, and historical Jews. The small amount of Hebrew literature written in America today is generally penned by and for Israelis" (Benor, "Do American Jews?" 241–42). There is no small controversy as to whether or not modern Hebrew should be regarded as a Jewish language. I am proposing with increasing fervor the cultivation of Judeo-Hebrew, indeed, a Jewish language of which one component (analogous to the Spanish, for instance, in *Judezmo*) is modern Hebrew.

22. See Fishman, "The Sociology of Jewish Languages": "I define as 'Jewish' any language that is phonologically, morpho-syntactically, lexico-semantically or orthographically different from that of non-Jewish sociocultural networks and that has some demonstrably unique function in the role-repertoire of a Jewish sociocultural network, which function is not normatively present in the role-repertoire of non-Jews and/or is not normatively discharged via varieties identical with those utilized by non-Jews" (4). In my view, Fishman has got this just right.

23. https://www.marxists.org/archive/trotsky/1940/xx/jewish.htm. The online Trotsky Archive.

24. Benor, "Do American Jews?" 234. Benor does *not* say exactly what I am saying here, but I take it that her descriptions support my perspective, even if she might (or might not) not.

25. I am grateful to Dr. Dine Matut and Professor Yitzhaq Niborsky for their help with these materials.

26. English adapted from the William Davidson digital edition of the Koren Noé Talmud, with commentary by Rabbi Adin Even-Israel Steinsaltz.

27. I wish especially to thank here Professor Yizhaq Niborsky, who supported with his knowledge and authority (and generosity) what were essentially educated guesses on my part.

28. Finkin, *A Rhetorical Conversation.*

29. Fanon, *Black Skin, White Masks,* 1–2.

30. Here is the much more beautiful but less veracious version by Barbara and Benjamin Harshav:

> Say, what does it mean, the rain?
> Say, what does it make me hear?—
> Its long drops on windowpanes
> Rolling down, tear after tear.
> And my boots are filled with holes,
> And the streets in mud do float;
> Soon the winter comes along—
> And I have no winter coat.

(Waiting for the World-to-Come . . . translated by Benjamin Harshav and Barbara Harshav, Facebook, https://www.facebook.com/yiddishkayt/posts/another-great-reyzen-song-may-ko-mashmo-lon-sung-beautifully-by-louis-dantohttps /424209277604467/ (accessed 22 June 2021).

The problem, as should be clear by now, is that the translation—quite close to the original semantically, prosodically, and even in rhyme scheme—completely misses the linguistic cultural import of the poem, the double translation with the linguistic translation of the first two lines of each stanza doubling the thematic translation from the House of Study to the street.

31. The transliteration has been adapted from a publication of the Hebrew Publishing Company, New York, 1915. I have only substituted the word *foist* [= fist] for the word *bank* [= bench] as the former appears in most versions of the song as published. The translation is mine. The text can be examined as well at https://www.ze mereshet.co.il/song.asp?id=10976. I wish especially to thank my colleague Professor Chana Kronfeld for her help with the Yiddish. Again, the beautiful translation by the Harshavs almost captures the sensibility of the poem:

> Say, what does it mean, my life?
> Say, what does it make me hear?

In my youth, to rot and wither,
To grow old and disappear.
Eat in strangers' homes in turn
Sleep on fists till they grow numb,
Killing This-World day by day.

(Waiting for the World-to-Come)

Beautiful indeed, but again, it sacrifices much for the beauty, namely, the relation between the first two lines, which is the essence for interpreting, as shown here. From line 3 on, it is perfect, but so much has been lost on the way there.

32. "I still adhere to the great Yiddish modernist Yankev Glatshteyn's admonishment that *Yiddishkayt* without a Jewish language—Glatshteyn puns here on *Yiddish* as an adjective meaning 'Jewish'—is the cloying 'honey-margarine' or the soft 'soaked challah' that toothless Jewish consumers of culture gum in order to get an ersatz, feelgood taste of the complex, intellectually challenging Jewish cultural heritage they have abandoned and now want nostalgically to invoke, but without being bothered to actually study it" (Kronfeld, "The Joint Literary Historiography of Hebrew and Yiddish," 1616).

33. Benor, "Do American Jews?" 245. Finkin, *A Rhetorical Conversation*, is excellent on this as well.

34. Benor, "Do American Jews?" 245.

35. Benor, "Do American Jews?" 231.

36. Benor, "Do American Jews?" 266.

37. See on this the lovely essay by Dara Horn, "The Future of Yiddish—in English."

38. Benor, "Do American Jews?" 241–42.

39. Ram, "Zionist Historiography," 97.

Chapter 8. What Was I Thinking?

1. Lapidot, *Jews out of the Question.*

2. Lapidot, *Jews out of the Question,* 9.

3. An epistemic object, to use Lapidot's terminology, whether valuable object or not, can be a subject for debate, of course.

4. After careful analysis of the texts on anti-Semitism of the Frankfurt critical theorists Adorno and Horkheimer, Lapidot concludes that for them, "the refutation of anti-Semitism does not lie in giving an opposite, positive answer to the Jewish Question, but in abolishing the question, which means abolishing the reference to

the Jews, both as perception and signification, i.e., making Jews disappear" (*Jews out of the Question*, 59).

5. Lapidot, *Jews out of the Question*, 9.

6. Sartre, *Anti-Semite and Jew*.

7. For instance, Boyarin, *Carnal Israel* begins by adopting as its title Augustine's indictment of the Jews as "carnal." Its opening sentence is, if I remember correctly, "Augustine got it right."

8. Burden-Stelly, "Cold War Culturalism," 218.

9. Pianko, *Zionism and the Roads Not Taken*, 27.

10. See Kletenick and Neis, "What's the Matter with Jewish Studies?"

11. Sharp, *Loon*, 28.

Bibliography

Anderson, Benedict. *Imagined Communities: Reflections on the Origin and Spread of Nationalism.* London: Verso, 1983.

Anidjar, Gil. *Blood: A Critique of Christianity.* Religion, Culture, and Public Life. New York: Columbia University Press, 2014.

———. "Secularism." *Critical Inquiry* 33 (2006): 52–77.

———. "We Have Never Been Jewish: An Essay in Asymmetric Hematology." In *Jewish Blood: Reality and Metaphor in History, Religion, and Culture,* edited by Mitchell B. Hart, 31–56. Routledge Jewish Studies Series. London: Routledge, 2009.

Anzi, Menashe. "Yemenite Jews in the Red Sea Trade and the Development of a New Diaspora." *Northeast African Studies* 17, no. 1 (2017): 79–100.

Appiah, Kwame Anthony. *Cosmopolitanism: Ethics in a World of Strangers.* Issues of Our Time. New York: Norton, 2006.

———. *The Ethics of Identity.* Princeton, N.J.: Princeton University Press, 2005.

———. Foreword to *Black Skin, White Masks,* by Frantz Fanon. Translated by Richard Philcox. 1952. Reprint, New York: Grove, 2008.

Arendt, Hannah. *The Jew as Pariah: Jewish Identity and Politics in the Modern Age.* Edited and with an introduction by Ron H. Feldman. New York: Grove, 1978.

Asad, Talal. *Formations of the Secular: Christianity, Islam, Modernity.* Cultural Memory in the Present. Stanford, Calif.: Stanford University Press, 2003.

———. *Genealogies of Religion: Discipline and Reasons of Power in Christianity and Islam.* Baltimore, Md.: Johns Hopkins University Press, 1993.

Aumüller, Alexander. "Unofficial Translation of 151 Ns 169/11." https://www
.dur.ac.uk/resources/ilm/CircumcisionJudgmentLGCologne-
7May20121.pdf.

Barbu, Daniel. "Discussion of *Judaism: The Genealogy of a Modern Notion*,
by Daniel Boyarin." *Quest: Issues in Contemporary Jewish History* 17
(2020): 192–201.

Baron, Salo Wittmayer. *Christian Era: The First Five Centuries*. Vol. 2 of *A
Social and Religious History of the Jews*. 2nd ed. Philadelphia: Jewish Publication Society, 1952.

Barton, Carlin A., and Daniel Boyarin. *Imagine No Religion: How Modern
Categories Hide Ancient Realities*. Bronx, N.Y.: Fordham University
Press, 2016.

Batnitzky, Leora. *How Judaism Became a Religion: An Introduction to Modern
Jewish Thought*. Princeton, N.J.: Princeton University Press, 2011.

Baumann, Martin. "Diaspora: Genealogies of Semantics and Transcultural
Comparison." *Numen* 47, no. 3 (2000): 313–37.

Benor, Sarah Bunin. "Do American Jews Speak a Jewish Language?" *Jewish
Quarterly Review* 99, no. 2 (2009): 230–69.

———. "Towards a New Understanding of Jewish Language in the Twenty-
First Century." *Religion Compass* 2, no. 6 (2008): 1062–80.

Bernasconi, Robert. "The Assumption of Negritude: Aimé Césaire, Frantz
Fanon, and the Vicious Circle of Racial Politics." *Parallax* 8, no. 2
(2002): 69–83.

———. "The European Knows and Does Not Know: Fanon's Response to
Sartre." In *Frantz Fanon's "Black Skin, White Masks": New Interdisciplin-
ary Essays*, edited by Max Silverman, 100–111. Manchester, U.K.: Manchester University Press, 2012.

Bevir, Mark. "On Tradition." *Humanitas* 13, no. 2 (2000): 28–53.

Bhabha, Homi K. "Of Mimicry and Men: The Ambivalence of Colonial
Discourse." *October* 28 (1984): 125–33.

Boyarin, Daniel. "Anna O(Rthodox): Bertha Pappenheim and the Making
of Jewish Feminism." "Experience, Representation, and Gender." Special issue, *Bulletin of the John Rylands Library* 83, no. 3 (Autumn 1998):
65–87.

———. *Carnal Israel: Reading Sex in Talmudic Culture.* The New Historicism: Studies in Cultural Poetics, vol. 25. Berkeley: University of California Press, 1993.

———. "The Colonial Drag: Zionism, Gender, and Colonial Mimicry." In *The Pre-occupation of Postcolonial Studies,* edited by Kalpana Seshadri-Crooks and Fawzia Afzal-Kahn, 234–65. Durham. N.C.: Duke University Press, 2000.

———. *Judaism: The Genealogy of a Modern Notion.* Key Words for Jewish Studies. New Brunswick, N.J.: Rutgers University Press, 2018.

———. *A Radical Jew: Paul and the Politics of Identity.* Contraversions: Critical Studies in Jewish Literature, Culture, and Society. Berkeley: University of California Press, 1994.

———. *A Traveling Homeland: The Babylonian Talmud as Diaspora.* Divinations. Philadelphia: University of Pennsylvania Press, 2015.

———. *Unheroic Conduct: The Rise of Heterosexuality and the Invention of the Jewish Man.* Contraversions: Critical Studies in Jewish Literature, Culture, and Society. Berkeley & Los Angeles: University of California Press, 1997.

Boyarin, Daniel, and Jonathan Boyarin. "Diaspora: Generation and the Ground of Jewish Identity." *Critical Inquiry* 19, no. 4 (Summer 1993): 693–725.

Boyarin, Jonathan. "Voices around the Text: The Ethnography of Reading at Mesivta Tifereth Jerusalem." *Cultural Anthropology* 4, no. 4 (1989): 399–421. https://www.jstor.org/stable/656249.

———. *Yeshiva Days: Learning on the Lower East Side.* Princeton, N.J.: Princeton University Press, 2020.

Boyarin, Jonathan, and Daniel Boyarin. *Powers of Diaspora: Two Essays on the Relevance of Jewish Culture.* Minneapolis: University of Minnesota Press, 2002.

Breckenridge, Carol A., Sheldon Pollock, Homi K. Bhabha, and Dipesh Chakrabarty, eds. *Cosmopolitanism.* A Millennial Quartet Book. Durham, N.C.: Duke University Press, 2002.

Burden-Stelly, Charisse. "Cold War Culturalism and African Diaspora Theory: Some Theoretical Sketches." *Souls* 19, no. 2 (2017): 213–37.

Butler, Judith. *Frames of War: When Is Life Grievable?* London: Verso, 2009.

———. "Performative Agency." *Journal of Cultural Economy* 3, no. 2 (2010): 147–61. DOI: 10.1080/17530350.2010.494117.

Césaire, Aimé. *Discourse on Colonialism.* Translated by Joan Pinkham. New York: Monthly Review Press, 2000.

Chatterjee, Partha. *The Nation and Its Fragments: Colonial and Postcolonial Histories.* Princeton Studies in Culture/Power/History. Princeton, N.J.: Princeton University Press, 1993.

Cheah, Pheng. "Introduction Part II: The Cosmopolitical Today." In *Cosmopolitics Thinking and Feeling beyond the Nation*, by Pheng Cheah, Bruce Robbins, and Social Text Collective, 20–41. Minneapolis: University of Minnesota Press, 1998.

Clifford, James. Review of *Orientalism*, by Edward W. Said. *History and Theory* 19, no. 2 (1980): 204–23.

Cohen, Robin. *Global Diasporas: An Introduction.* 2nd ed. Global Diasporas. London: Routledge, 2008.

Collini, Stefan. "Living in the Love of the Common People." Review of *Out of the Ordinary*, by Marc Stears. *Times Literary Supplement*, 8 January 2021, 10–11.

Connelly, John. *From Enemy to Brother: The Revolution in Catholic Teaching on the Jews, 1933–1965.* Cambridge, Mass.: Harvard University Press, 2012.

Conway, Timothy. "Spiritual Humor." https://www.enlightened-spirituality.org/Spiritual_Humor.html.

Cooper, Becky. *We Keep the Dead Close: A Murder at Harvard and a Half Century of Silence.* New York: Grand Central, 2020.

Dagan, Haggai. "Blood and Myth in the Thought of Franz Rosenzweig." In *Jewish Blood: Reality and Metaphor in History, Religion, and Culture*, edited by Mitchell B. Hart, 152–59. London: Routledge, 2009.

———. "The Motif of Blood and Procreation in Franz Rosenzweig." *Association for Jewish Studies Review* 26, no. 2 (November 2002): 241–49.

Dimitrovsky, Hayyim Zalman. "Do the Jews Have a Middle Ages?" [In Hebrew.] In *Meḥkarim Be-Mada'e Ha-Yahadut*, edited by Moshe Bar Asher, 257–65. Yerushalayim: Hebrew University, 1986.

Dinur, Ben Zion. *Israel and the Diaspora*. With an introduction by Yitzshak Baer. Philadelphia: Jewish Publication Society of America, 1969.

Dirks, Nicholas B. "The Policing of Tradition: Colonialism and Anthropology in Southern India." *Comparative Studies in Society and History* 39, no. 1 (1997): 182–212.

Dolgopolski, Sergey. *What Is Talmud? The Art of Disagreement*. New York: Fordham University Press, 2008.

Drory, Rina. *Models and Contacts: Arabic Literature and Its Impact on Medieval Jewish Culture*. Brill's Series in Jewish Studies, vol. 25. Leiden: Brill, 2000.

Du Bois, W. E. B. *Black Reconstruction in America: An Essay toward a History of the Part Which Black Folk Played in the Attempt to Reconstruct Democracy in America, 1860–1880*. With an introduction by David Levering Lewis. New York: Oxford University Press, 2007.

———. *The World and Africa: An Inquiry into the Part Which Africa Has Played in World History*. New York: Viking, 1947.

Epstein, Brian. "Social Ontology." In *The Stanford Encyclopedia of Philosophy*, edited by Edward N. Zalta. 2018. https://plato.stanford.edu/archives/sum2018/entries/social-ontology/.

Fanon, Frantz. *Black Skin, White Masks*. Translated by Richard Philcox. With a foreword by Kwame Anthony Appiah. 1952. Reprint, New York: Grove, 2008.

Fateh-Maghadam, Bijan. "Criminalizing Male Circumcision? Case Note: Landgerich Cologne, Judgement of 7 May 2012—No. 151 Ns 169//." *German Law Journal* 13, no. 92012 (2012): 1131–45.

Finkin, Jordan D. *A Rhetorical Conversation: Jewish Discourse and Modern Yiddish Literature*. University Park: Pennsylvania State University Press, 2010.

Fishman, Joshua A. "The Sociology of Jewish Languages from a General Sociolinguistic Point of View." In *Readings in the Sociology of Jewish Languages*, edited by Joshua A. Fishman, 3–21. Contributions to the Sociology of Jewish Languages, vol. 1. Leiden: Brill, 1985.

Fishman, Talya. *Becoming the People of the Talmud: Oral Torah as Written Tradition in Medieval Jewish Cultures*. Jewish Culture and Contexts. Philadelphia: University of Pennsylvania Press, 2011.

Fitzgerald, Timothy. *Discourse on Civility and Barbarity: A Critical History of Religion and Related Categories.* New York: Oxford University Press, 2007.

——. *The Ideology of Religious Studies.* New York: Oxford University Press, 2000.

Flood, Finbarr B. *Objects of Translation: Material Culture and Medieval "Hindu-Muslim" Encounter.* Princeton, N.J.: Princeton University Press, 2009.

Gafni, Isaiah. "Babylonian Rabbinic Culture." In *Cultures of the Jews: A New History*, edited by David Biale, 224–97. New York: Schocken Books, 2002.

——. *Land, Center and Diaspora Jewish Constructs in Late Antiquity.* Journal for the Study of the Pseudepigrapha. Supplement series. Sheffield, U.K.: Sheffield Academic Press, 1997.

Gilman, Sander L. *Jewish Self-Hatred: Anti-Semitism and the Hidden Language of the Jews.* Baltimore, Md.: Johns Hopkins University Press, 1986.

Gitelman, Zvi, ed. *Religion or Ethnicity? Jewish Identities in Evolution.* New Brunswick, N.J.: Rutgers University Press, 2009.

Gruen, Erich S. *Diaspora: Jews amidst Greeks and Romans.* Cambridge, Mass.: Harvard University Press, 2002.

Hacking, Ian. "Making Up People." In *Reconstructing Individualism: Autonomy, Individuality, and the Self in Western Thought*, edited by Thomas C. Heller and Christine Brooke-Rose. Stanford, Calif.: Stanford University Press, 1986.

Ho, Engseng. *The Graves of Tarim: Genealogy and Mobility across the Indian Ocean.* The California World History Library. Berkeley: University of California Press, 2006.

Hobsbawm, E. J. *Nations and Nationalism since 1780: Programme, Myth, Reality.* Cambridge: Cambridge University Press, 1992.

Hollinger, David A. *Postethnic America: Beyond Multiculturalism.* New York: Basic Books; London: Perseus Running, 2005.

Horn, Dara. "The Future of Yiddish—in English: Field Notes from the New Ashkenaz." *Jewish Quarterly Review* 96, no. 4 (2006): 471–80.

Kant, Immanuel. "Religion within the Bounds of Bare Reason." *Early Modern Texts.* https://www.earlymoderntexts.com/assets/pdfs/kant1793.pdf.

Kelley, Robin D. G. "A Poetics of Anticolonialism." Introduction to *Discourse on Colonialism*, by Aimé Césaire. Translated by Joan Pinkham. New York: Monthly Review Press, 2000.

Kletenick, Gilah, and Rafael Rachel Neis. "What's the Matter with Jewish Studies? Sexism, Harassment, and Neoliberalism for Starters." *Religion Dispatches*, 19 April 2021.

Kronfeld, Chana. "The Joint Literary Historiography of Hebrew and Yiddish." In *Languages of Modern Jewish Cultures: Comparative Perspectives*, edited by Joshua L. Miller, Anita Norich, and Chana Kronfeld, 15–35. Ann Arbor: University of Michigan Press, 2016.

Lapidot, El'ad. *Jews out of the Question: A Critique of Anti-Anti-Semitism.* Philosophy and Race. Albany: State University of New York Press, 2020.

Leuba, James Henry. *A Psychological Study of Religion: Its Origin, Function, and Future.* 1912. Reprint, New York: AMS Press, 1969.

Levy, André, and Alex Weingrod, eds. *Homelands and Diasporas: Holy Lands and Other Places.* Stanford, Calif.: Stanford University Press, 2005.

Lieberman, Saul. *Greek in Jewish Palestine Studies in the Life and Manners of Jewish Palestine in the II–IV Centuries C.E.* New York: Jewish Theological Seminary of America, 1942.

Lyall, Sarah. "British High Court Says School's Ethnic-Based Admissions Policy Is Illegal." *New York Times*, 16 December 2009, https://www.nytimes.com/2009/12/17/world/europe/17britain.html.

Mahmood, Saba, and Peter G. Danchin. "Immunity or Regulation? Antinomies of Religious Freedom." *South Atlantic Quarterly* 113, no. 1 (2014): 129–59.

Memmi, Albert. "The Impossible Life of Frantz Fanon." Translated by Thomas Cassirer and G. Michael Twomey. *Massachusetts Review* 14, no. 1 (Winter 1973): 9–39.

Mendes-Flohr, Paul. *Cultural Disjunctions: Post-traditional Jewish Identities.* Chicago: University of Chicago Press, 2021.

Michaels, Walter Benn. "Race into Culture: A Critical Genealogy of Cultural Identity." *Critical Inquiry* 18, no. 4 (Summer 1992): 655–86.

Moten, Fred. *Black and Blur.* Durham, N.C.: Duke University Press, 2017.

———. *Stolen Life.* Durham, N.C.: Duke University Press, 2018.

———. *The Universal Machine*. Durham, N.C.: Duke University Press, 2018.

Moyn, Samuel. "From Communist to Muslim: European Human Rights, the Cold War, and Religious Liberty." *South Atlantic Quarterly* 131 (2014): 63–86.

Mufti, Aamir R. *Enlightenment in the Colony: The Jewish Question and the Crisis of Postcolonial Culture*. Princeton, N.J.: Princeton University Press, 2007.

Newman, Zelda Kahan. "The Jewish Sound of Speech: Talmudic Chant, Yiddish Intonation and the Origins of Early Ashkenaz." *Jewish Quarterly Review* 90, nos. 3/4 (2000): 293–336.

Nussbaum, Martha C., and respondents. *For Love of Country: Debating the Limits of Patriotism*. Edited by Joshua Cohen. Boston: Beacon, 1996.

Okiji, Fumi. *Jazz as Critique: Adorno and Black Expression Revisited*. Stanford, Calif.: Stanford University Press, 2018.

Ophir, Adi, and Ishay Rosen-Zvi. *Goy: Israel's Multiple Others and the Birth of the Gentile*. Oxford: Oxford University Press, 2018.

Pandey, Gyanendra. "In Defense of the Fragment: Writing about Hindu-Muslim Riots in India Today." *Representations* 37 (1992): 27–55.

Pearce, Laurie E., and Cornelia Wunsch. *Documents of Judean Exiles and West Semites in Babylonia in the Collection of David Sofer*. Cornell University Studies in Assyriology and Sumerology (CUSAS), 2014.

Pianko, Noam. *Jewish Peoplehood: An American Innovation*. Key Words in Jewish Studies, vol. 6. New Brunswick, N.J.: Rutgers University Press, 2015.

———. *Zionism and the Roads Not Taken: Rawidowicz, Kaplan, Kohn*. The Modern Jewish Experience. Bloomington: Indiana University Press, 2010.

Rabaka, Reiland. *Forms of Fanonism: Frantz Fanon's Critical Theory and the Dialectics of Decolonization*. Lanham, Md.: Lexington Books, 2010.

———. *The Negritude Movement: W. E. B. Du Bois, Leon Damas, Aime Césaire, Leopold Senghor, Frantz Fanon, and the Evolution of an Insurgent Idea*. Critical Africana Studies. Lanham, Md.: Lexington Books, 2015.

Rabinow, Paul. "Representations Are Social Facts: Modernity and Postmodernity in Anthropology." In *Writing Culture: The Poetics and Politics of Ethnography: A School of American Research Advanced Seminar*, edited by James Clifford and George E. Marcus, 234–61. Berkeley: University of California Press, 1986.

Ram, Uri. "Zionist Historiography and the Invention of Modern Jewish Nationhood: The Case of Ben Zion Dinur." *History and Memory, Israeli Historiography Revisited* 7, no. 1 (1995): 91–124.

Raz-Krakotzkin, Amnon. "Exile within Sovereignty: Critique of 'The Negation of Exile' in Israeli Culture." In *The Scaffolding of Sovereignty: Global and Aesthetic Perspectives on the History of a Concept*, edited by Zvi Ben-Dor Benite, Stefanos Geroulanos, and Nicole Jerr, 395–420. New York: Columbia University Press, 2017.

———. "Exile within Sovereignty: Toward a Critique of the 'Negation of Exile' in Israeli Culture." [In Hebrew.] *Theory and Criticism: An Israeli Forum* 4 (Autumn 1993): 23–56, 184–86 (English summary).

Renan, Ernest. "What Is a Nation?" In *Nation and Narration*, edited by Homi K. Bhabha, 8–22. London: Routledge, 1990.

Ritchie, Katherine. "Neither Fate nor Fiction: Finding Social Groups in Networks of Relations." *The Philosopher*, no. 107 (1992): 11–14.

Robbins, Bruce. "Comparative Cosmopolitanisms." *Social Text* 31/32 (1992): 169–86.

———. "Introduction Part I: Actually Existing Cosmopolitanism." In *Cosmopolitics Thinking and Feeling beyond the Nation*, by Pheng Cheah, Bruce Robbins, and Social Text Collective, 1–19. Minneapolis: University of Minnesota Press, 1998.

Rosenzweig, Franz. *The Star of Redemption: Translated from the 2d Ed. of 1930 by William W. Hallo*. New York: Holt, Rinehart and Winston, 1971.

Rubenstein, Jeffrey. "Addressing the Attributes of the Land of Israel: An Analysis of Bavli Ketubot 110b–112a." [In Hebrew, with English summary.] In *Center and Diaspora: The Land of Israel and the Diaspora in the Second Temple, Mishna and Talmud Periods* [in Hebrew], edited by Isaiah M. Gafni, 159–88. Yerushalayim: Merkaz Zalman Shazar le-toldot Yisrael, 2004.

Sahlins, Peter. *Boundaries: The Making of France and Spain in the Pyrenees*. Berkeley: University of California Press, 1989.

Salaymeh, Lena, and Shai Lavi. "Religion Is Secularized Tradition: Jewish and Muslim Circumcisions in Germany." *Oxford Journal of Legal Studies* 41, no. 2 (2021): 431–58.

Saler, Benson. *Conceptualizing Religion: Immanent Anthropologists, Transcendent Natives, and Unbounded Categories.* Studies in the History of Religions, vol. 56. Leiden: Brill, 1993.

Sand, Shlomo. *The Invention of the Jewish People.* Translated by Yael Lotan. London: Verso, 2009.

Sartre, Jean-Paul. *Anti-Semite and Jew.* Translated by George G. Becker. New York: Schocken Books, 1946.

———. *Black Orpheus.* Translated by S. W. Allen. Paris: Présence Africaine, 1976.

Saussy, Haun. *Are We Comparing Yet? On Standards, Justice, and Incomparability.* Bielelfeld: Bielelfeld University Press, 2019.

Sharp, Henry S. *Loon: Memory, Meaning, and Reality in a Northern Dene Community.* Lincoln: University of Nebraska Press, 2001.

Shumsky, Dmitry. *Between Prague and Jerusalem: Prague Zionists and the Origins of the Idea of Binational State in Palestine.* [In Hebrew.] Jerusalem: Shazar Center and Leo Baeck Institute Jerusalem, 2010.

———. *Beyond the Nation-State: The Zionist Political Imagination from Pinsker to Ben-Gurion.* New Haven, Conn.: Yale University Press, 2018.

Spolsky, Bernard, and Sarah Bunin Benor. "Jewish Languages." In *Encyclopedia of Language and Linguistics*, edited by Keith Brown, 6:120–24. Amsterdam: Elsevier, 2006.

Stern, Eliyahu. *Jewish Materialism: The Intellectual Revolution of the 1870s.* New Haven, Conn.: Yale University Press, 2018.

Tzuberi, Hannah. " 'Reforesting' Jews: The German State and the Construction of 'New German Judaism.' " *Jewish Studies Quarterly* 27 (2020).

Walzer, Michael. "Anti-Zionism and Anti-Semitism." *Dissent*, Fall 2019, https://www.dissentmagazine.org/article/anti-zionism-and-anti-semitism.

Weinreich, Max. *History of the Yiddish Language.* Translated by Shlomo Noble with the assistance of Joshua A. Fishman and the editorial assistance of Paul Glasser. Yale Language Series. New Haven, Conn.: Yale University Press, 2008.

Werbner, Penina. "The Place Which Is Diaspora: Citizenship, Religion, and Gender in the Making of Chaordic Transnationalism." In *Homelands and Diasporas: Holy Lands and Other Places*, edited by André Levy and Alex Weingrod, 29–48. Stanford, Calif.: Stanford University Press, 2005.

Whitebook, Joel. *Freud: An Intellectual Biography*. Cambridge: Cambridge University Press, 2017.

Wilderson, Frank B., III. *Afropessimism*. New York: Liveright, 2020.

Williams, Patricia. "To the North: Race, Migration and Violence in the United States of America." *Times Literary Supplement*, 23 April 2021, 7–8.

Wimpfheimer, Barry Scott. *The "Talmud": A Biography*. Lives of Great Religious Books. Princeton, N.J.: Princeton University Press, 2018.

Wolfson, Elliot R. *The Duplicity of Philosophy's Shadow: Heidegger, Nazism, and the Jewish Other*. New York: Columbia University Press, 2018.

Yadgar, Yaacov. "Tradition." *Human Studies* 36 (2013): 451–70.

Zgusta, Ladislav. "Diaspora: The Past in the Present." *Studies in the Linguistic Sciences* 31, no. 1 (2001): 291–97.

Acknowledgments

I wish to thank the following for various modes of interaction with earlier versions of these texts (only I am responsible for remaining infelicities): Jonathan Boyarin, Ishay Rosen-Zvi, Haggai Dagan, Maya Kronfeld, Fumi Okiji, Fellows of the Centre for the Study of Religion and Society (UVIC), Gil Anidjar, Haun Saussy, Ato Quayson, Amnon Raz-Krakotzkin, El'ad Lapidot, anonymous readers for CI and boundary 2, Ari Resnikoff, Carlin Barton, Yitzhaq Niborsky, Dine Matut, Elli Stern, Elliot Wolfson, Susan Griffin, Marc Rastoin, S.J., Chana Kronfeld, and Vincent Bynack.

Index

Abraham, 15, 31, 54, 94
Adeni (saint), 95–96
Adorno, Theodor, 125, 156n4
affinity, 49
Ahad Ha'am. *See* Ginzberg, Asher
Ahashverus, 30
Anderson, Benedict, 51–54, 141n9
Anidjar, Gil, 38, 49–50, 55, 58
anti-anti-Semitism, 124–26
anti-Semitism: anti-Zionism confused
    with, 11, 137n10; Arendt and, 110–11;
    critiques of, 125–26; disappearance
    of Jews as proposed solution for,
    65, 110, 124–26, 156n4; Herzl's
    Zionism as response to, 78; Jewish
    identity constituted through,
    65–66, 125, 140n30; Jews blamed
    for, 65, 110; language and, 110;
    negrophobia associated with,
    63–64, 67
anti-Zionism: anti-Semitism
    distinguished from, 11, 137n10;
    Arendt and, 110–11; author's
    position of, ix, 75–76; and Jews as a
    religion, 1–2, 11, 37–38; Pinsker as
    precursor of, 85
Anzi, Menashe, 90
Appiah, Kwame Anthony, 18–21, 23,
    51, 61, 62, 96–97, 134n35

Aramaic, 28, 30, 113–16, 119, 154n20
Arendt, Hannah, 98, 110–11
Ashkenazic Jews, xi, 33, 35, 90, 111
assimilation, 60, 61, 77, 85
Augustine, 126

Babylonia, 26, 28–31, 99–100, 104–5
Babylonian Talmud, 100–102, 113,
    135n11
Baer, Itzhak, 150n2
Baumann, Martin, 91–92
belief. *See* faith
belonging: cosmopolitanism
    antithetical to, 17, 23–24, 97; to
    diaspora, 97; family as exemplar of,
    47–48; Jewish, 42, 46–48, 53–58; to
    a nation, ix, 24; performance of,
    56–58
Ben-Gurion, David, 32
Benor, Sarah Bunin, 119–22, 150n5
Bernasconi, Robert, 62, 142n2, 144n11,
    145n26
Bevir, Mark, 98–99
Bhabha, Homi, 148n4
Biddick, Kathleen, 13
bilingualism, 149n15
Black Diaspora, 91–92
Black Lives Matter (BLM), 17, 70,
    127, 152n23